D1364275

High Priest
and
Coming King

High Priest
and
Coming King

Maurice Hoppe, MA

Bible and Systematic Theology
Potomac University

Copyright © 2009 by Maurice Hoppe, MA.

Library of Congress Control Number: 2009903241
ISBN: Hardcover   978-1-4415-2544-4
                   Softcover   978-1-4415-2543-7

All rights reserved. No part of this book may be reproduced or transmitted in any form or by any means, electronic or mechanical, including photocopying, recording, or by any information storage and retrieval system, without permission in writing from the copyright owner.

This book was printed in the United States of America, by Mennonite Press, Inc., Newton, KS 67114.

To order additional copies of this book, contact:
Steps to Life
PO Box 782828
Wichita, KS 67278
1-800-843-8788
www.stepstolife.org
info@stepstolife.org

Contents

Preface

This book, dear reader, is published to provide for you an explanation of the great controversy between Christ and Satan that has been in progress for some 6,000 years. The special focus of this presentation is on the closing scenes of this controversy. We have already entered the closing events in the history of this world. In our hearts, we know it, and we know that we are participators—actors—in this conflict.

We will touch briefly on how the controversy began and cover the major events of this controversy as it has developed through the ages. We will answer questions such as, how do I relate to it? What is my responsibility in it? How can I be sure I am on the right side of this controversy? What are the great principles involved? How long will it continue?

This book will focus especially on the great second advent movement that began in the early part of the nineteenth century in the United States with the Millerite movement. Why has Jesus been so long in coming? Where are we at the present time in the final conflict? We will cover in detail the remaining events to occur as explained by the prophets of God.

> Surely the Sovereign LORD does nothing without revealing
> his plan to his servants the prophets. (Amos 3:7)

We want to understand as much as we can about what God has revealed to us through inspired writings.

It is the aim of this book to provide you with a clear explanation of why we are in such a troubled world today. This book has been prepared and reviewed by men who have had long experience in the great second advent movement. Our earnest desire is that the information in this book will help you to be prepared to meet your Lord in peace when He returns. We believe that the "secret of the Lord is with them that fear Him; and he will shew them his covenant" (Ps. 25:14, KJV).

Two great themes will be developed in the presentation of this controversy. The first and foremost is the great love that God the Father and His Son Jesus Christ have for the fallen race. God has revealed this love to us through the system of sacrifices and the sanctuary services as conducted in the sanctuary on earth during the time of the Old Testament. This wonderful love for fallen man is further developed in the death of Jesus on the cross of Calvary and His ministry in the heavenly sanctuary since His ascension for the removal of sins that have been confessed and forsaken.

The second theme will present the work of Satan and his agents—the apostate churches—in their effort to keep the knowledge of this wonderful ministry of Jesus and the hope of salvation from the people of the world. In the closing scenes of the conflict, the atoning blood of Christ in the most holy place of the sanctuary in heaven will be the great hope and anchor for the true people of God.

> For God so loved the world that he gave his one and only [begotten] Son, that whoever believes in him shall not perish but have eternal life. (John 3:16)

In this conflict, no one can be neutral. All will have to take their stand on one side or the other. Your decision will determine your eternal destiny.

This manuscript reveals the eternal and glorious victory of good over evil, right over wrong, light over darkness, joy over sorrow, hope over despair, glory over shame, love over vindictive hate.

Bible texts quoted in this book are from the New International Version except as otherwise noted or when included within another quotation. Below is a list of other versions used and their abbreviations.

KJV   King James Version
MKJV   Modern King James Version
MNT   Montgomery's New Testament
NASB   New American Standard Bible
NKJV   New King James Version
NRSV   New Revised Standard Version
RSV   Revised Standard Version
WNT   Weymouth's New Testament

It is our earnest prayer that this book will help you to look to Jesus as your High Priest and coming King of kings.

John J. Grosboll, Director
> Steps to Life
>> *historic@stepstolife.org*
>> *www.stepstolife.org*

Maurice Hoppe, Director of Training Programs
> Steps to Life
>> Training Program for Ministers and Church Leaders
>> Preparing for the Final Conflict
>> *mauricehoppe@stepstolife.org*
> Revelation Ministry
>> *hoppe@revelationministry.com*

Domingo Nuñez, Director of Outreach
> Steps to Life
>> *domingonunez@stepstolife.org*

1

The Great Controversy
between Christ and Satan Begins

> A great and wondrous sign appeared in heaven: a woman
> clothed with the sun, with the moon under her feet and a crown
> of twelve stars on her head.
>
> —Revelation 12:1

In the scriptures, the symbol of a woman is used to represent a church. When she is depicted as being pure, modest, and refined, she represents the true church of Christ. But when she is seen as a harlot, she represents an apostate church.

The beautiful woman pictured in this text is clothed with the sun. "For the Lord God is a sun" and "for you who revere My name, the sun of righteousness will rise with healing in its wings" (Ps. 84:11; Mal. 4:2). She typifies a pure, holy church clothed in the righteous character of Christ. She is standing on the moon. As the moon reflects the light of the sun, so this pure woman reflects the righteous character of Jesus.

"Then another sign appeared in heaven: an enormous red dragon with seven heads and ten horns and seven crowns on his heads." This dragon is "that ancient serpent called the devil, or Satan" (Rev. 12:3, 9).

Satan had occupied a very high position in heaven. Ezekiel describes the position this highly exalted guardian cherub held in heaven prior to his rebellion.

> You were the model of perfection, full of wisdom and
> perfect in beauty. You were in Eden, the garden of God; every
> precious stone adorned you: ruby, topaz and emerald, chrysolite,
> onyx and jasper, sapphire, turquoise and beryl. Your settings and
> mountings were made of gold; on the day you were created they

> were prepared. You were anointed as a guardian cherub, for so I ordained you. You were on the holy mount of God; you walked among the fiery stones. You were blameless in your ways from the day you were created. (Ezek. 28:12-15)

This glorious being was created by the hand of God and appointed as the guardian angel, the commander of the hosts of heaven. He stood in the very presence of the God of the universe and His Son Jesus Christ. He was called Lucifer, the "morning star, son of the dawn" (Isa. 14:12).

But a change took place in the mind and thinking of this commander of the angelic host. Isaiah exclaims,

> How you have fallen from heaven, O morning star, son of the dawn! . . . you who once laid low the nations! You said in your heart, "I will ascend to heaven; I will raise my throne above the stars of God; I will sit enthroned on the mount of assembly, on the utmost heights of the sacred mountain." (Isa. 14:12-13)
>
> You were blameless in your ways from the day you were created till wickedness was found in you. Your heart became proud on account of your beauty, and you corrupted your wisdom because of your splendor. (Ezek. 28:15, 17)

Thus a controversy developed in heaven between Christ and Lucifer. John says,

> And there was war in heaven. Michael and his angels fought against the dragon, and the dragon and his angels fought back. But he was not strong enough, and they lost their place in heaven. The great dragon was hurled down—that ancient serpent called the devil, or Satan, who leads the whole world astray. He was hurled to the earth, and his angels with him. (Rev. 12:7-9)

In describing this scene, the prophets write,

> Through your widespread trade you were filled with violence, and you sinned. So I drove you in disgrace from the mount of God, and I expelled you, O guardian cherub, from among the fiery stones. Your heart became proud on account of

your beauty, and you corrupted your wisdom because of your splendor. So I threw you to the earth; I made a spectacle of you before kings. By your many sins and dishonest trade you have desecrated your sanctuaries. (Ezek. 28:16-18)

You have been cast down to the earth, you who once laid low the nations! (Isa. 14:12)

This war caused a great loss to the kingdom of glory. Not only was the leader of the angelic hosts gone, but also one-third of the angels fell with him.

His tail swept a third of the stars out of the sky and flung them to the earth. (Rev. 12:4)

Not long after being cast out of heaven, Satan, the ancient serpent, went to the Garden of Eden where the newly created Adam and Eve were enjoying the beauties and bliss of their new life and home. After analyzing the situation, he began reasoning in his mind that if he could persuade Adam and Eve to disbelieve the Word of God, they would become his subjects, and he would then gain control of this earth. He soon developed a plan by which he hoped to obtain his objective. It is recorded for us by Moses.

Now the serpent was more crafty than any of the wild animals the LORD God had made. He said to the woman, "Did God really say, 'You must not eat from any tree in the garden'?" The woman said to the serpent, "We may eat fruit from the trees in the garden, but God did say, 'You must not eat fruit from the tree that is in the middle of the garden, and you must not touch it, or you will die.'" "You will not surely die," the serpent said to the woman. "For God knows that when you eat of it your eyes will be opened, and you will be like God, knowing good and evil." When the woman saw that the fruit of the tree was good for food and pleasing to the eye, and also desirable for gaining wisdom, she took some and ate it. She also gave some to her husband, who was with her, and he ate it. (Gen. 3:1-6)

Thus Adam and Eve also rebelled against God. So the great controversy that began in heaven spread to this world. This earth has since been the focal point of this war. Christ said to the serpent, "And I will put enmity between you and the woman, and between your offspring and hers; he will crush your head, and you will strike his heel" (Gen. 3:15). Since the fall of Adam and Eve, the controversy between the obedient and the disobedient, the followers of Jesus and the followers of Satan, has continued in this earth.

John gives us a brief snapshot of this war at the time of the first advent. Concerning the pure woman—the true church—he writes,

> She was pregnant and cried out in pain as she was about to give birth. The dragon stood in front of the woman who was about to give birth, so that he might devour her child the moment it was born. She gave birth to a son, a male child, . . . And her child was snatched up to God and to his throne. (Rev. 12:2, 4-5)

In these few words, John gives a brief account of the first advent of Christ. Right from His birth, Satan attempted to take the life of Jesus.

> When Herod realized that he had been outwitted by the Magi, he was furious, and he gave orders to kill all the boys in Bethlehem and its vicinity who were two years old and under, in accordance with the time he had learned from the Magi. (Matt. 2:16)

When Jesus had finished His work on earth, John says that "her child was snatched up to God and to his throne." In describing this event, the Bible says, "When he had led them out to the vicinity of Bethany, he lifted up his hands and blessed them. While he was blessing them, he left them and was taken up into heaven" (Luke 24:50-51). Again it reads, "After he said this, he was taken up before their very eyes, and a cloud hid him from their sight" (Acts 1:9).

In a war story, three things are generally explained in the beginning of the story—(1) the leader and people on the good side, (2) the leader and those on the bad side, and (3) a brief introduction to the plot. Thus far, we have found that Christ and His followers, represented by the pure woman, are on the good side in this conflict. The bad side is led by Satan, that enormous red dragon, the fallen angels, and those who work against Jesus.

John, in Revelation 12, gives a brief introduction to the plot of the controversy. Before we can understand the plot, we need to be aware of the issues involved. The newly organized Christian church was fulfilling the commission that Christ had given to them when He said they were to "go and make disciples of all nations, baptizing them in the name of the Father and of the Son and of the Holy Spirit, and teaching them to obey everything I have commanded you" (Matt. 28:19-20).

When Satan saw the success of this early Christian church in drawing people to Christ and taking them out of his control, he determined to stop their work.

"He pursued the woman who had given birth to the male child." "The woman fled into the desert to a place prepared for her by God, where she might be taken care of for 1,260 days."[1] "The woman was given the two wings of a great eagle, so that she might fly to the place prepared for her in the desert, where she would be taken care of for a time, times and half a time,[2] out of the serpent's reach." (Rev. 12:13, 6, 14)

The great red dragon, Satan, "is filled with fury, because he knows that his time is short." "From his mouth the serpent spewed water like a river, to overtake the woman and sweep her away with the torrent" (Rev. 12:12, 15). Through this long period of 1,260 years of persecution, the faithful believers "overcame him by the blood of the Lamb and by the word of their testimony; they did not love their lives so much as to shrink from death" (Rev. 12:11).

After the great red dragon had pursued the faithful church for 1,260 days (years), there was a remnant that he could not overcome. This dragon was enraged at the woman—the true church—"and went off to make war against the rest of her offspring—those who obey God's commandments and hold to the testimony of Jesus" (Rev. 12:17).

This plot reveals that there would be a long conflict between this pure woman—the true church—and the great red dragon. And at the end of time, the dragon would intensify his war against the woman. In the pages that follow, we will study the details of this war and the issues involved. We will also identify who is on each side of the war and how it will finally end.

---

1.   In prophecy, a day is used to represent a year (Num. 14:34; Ezek. 4:6).
2.   In prophecy, a time equals 360 days. Times equals 720 days. Half a time is 180 days. Therefore 1,260 days equals 1,260 years of prophetic time.

2

The Purpose of Sacrifices

After creating Adam and Eve on the sixth day of creation, God gave them the following instruction:

> And the LORD God commanded the man, "You are free to eat from any tree in the garden; but you must not eat from the tree of the knowledge of good and evil, for when you eat of it you will surely die." (Gen. 2:16-17)

Soon after Adam and Eve were created, the great red dragon, under the guise of a serpent, entered into the Garden of Eden. He entered into conversation with Eve, and through deception and lies, he persuaded her to partake of the forbidden fruit.

> When the woman saw that the fruit of the tree was good for food and pleasing to the eye, and also desirable for gaining wisdom, she took some and ate it. She also gave some to her husband, who was with her, and he ate it. (Gen. 3:6)

Adam and Eve sinned against the God of heaven by disobeying His express command not to eat of the forbidden fruit. Paul says that "the wages of sin is death" (Rom. 6:23). Through Adam and Eve, the whole human race has come under the power of sin, "for all have sinned and fall short of the glory of God" (Rom. 3:23).

> The fall of man filled all heaven with sorrow. The world that God had made was blighted with the curse of sin and inhabited by beings doomed to misery and death. There appeared no escape for those who had transgressed the law. Angels ceased

their songs of praise. Throughout the heavenly courts there was mourning for the ruin that sin had wrought.

The Son of God, heaven's glorious Commander, was touched with pity for the fallen race. His heart was moved with infinite compassion as the woes of the lost world rose up before Him. But divine love had conceived a plan whereby man might be redeemed. The broken law of God demanded the life of the sinner. In all the universe there was but one who could, in behalf of man, satisfy its claims. Since the divine law is as sacred as God Himself, only one equal with God could make atonement for its transgression. None but Christ could redeem fallen man from the curse of the law and bring him again into harmony with Heaven. Christ would take upon Himself the guilt and shame of sin—sin so offensive to a holy God that it must separate the Father and His Son. Christ would reach to the depths of misery to rescue the ruined race.

Before the Father He pleaded in the sinner's behalf, while the host of heaven awaited the result with an intensity of interest that words cannot express. Long continued was that mysterious communing—"the counsel of peace" (Zechariah 6:13) for the fallen sons of men. The plan of salvation had been laid before the creation of the earth; for Christ is "the Lamb slain from the foundation of the world" (Revelation 13:8); yet it was a struggle, even with the King of the universe, to yield up His Son to die for the guilty race. But "God so loved the world, that He gave His only-begotten Son, that whosoever believeth in Him should not perish, but have everlasting life." John 3:16. Oh, the mystery of redemption! the love of God for a world that did not love Him!" (*Patriarchs and Prophets*, 63-64)

God was to be manifest in Christ, "reconciling the world unto Himself." 2 Corinthians 5:19. Man had become so degraded by sin that it was impossible for him, in himself, to come into harmony with Him whose nature is purity and goodness. But Christ, after having redeemed man from the condemnation of the law, could impart divine power to unite with human effort. Thus by repentance toward God and faith in Christ the fallen children of Adam might once more become "sons of God." 1 John 3:2.

The plan by which alone man's salvation could be secured, involved all heaven in its infinite sacrifice. The angels could not rejoice as Christ opened before them the plan of redemption, for they saw that man's salvation must cost their loved Commander unutterable woe. In grief and wonder they listened to His words as He told them how He must descend from heaven's purity and peace, its joy and glory and immortal life, and come in contact with the degradation of earth, to endure its sorrow, shame, and death. He was to stand between the sinner and the penalty of sin; yet few would receive Him as the Son of God. He would leave His high position as the Majesty of heaven, appear upon earth and humble Himself as a man, and by His own experience become acquainted with the sorrows and temptations which man would have to endure. All this would be necessary in order that He might be able to succor [help] them that should be tempted. Hebrews 2:18. When His mission as a teacher should be ended, He must be delivered into the hands of wicked men and be subjected to every insult and torture that Satan could inspire them to inflict. He must die the cruelest of deaths, lifted up between the heavens and the earth as a guilty sinner. He must pass long hours of agony so terrible that angels could not look upon it, but would veil their faces from the sight. He must endure anguish of soul, the hiding of His Father's face, while the guilt of transgression—the weight of the sins of the whole world—should be upon Him. (ibid., 64)

With the adoption of the plan of salvation, a new kingdom was instituted called the kingdom of grace. The kingdom of grace is a most wonderful provision for the fallen human race, but it is provided at a very high cost. Only the blood of Christ could meet the demands required to provide saving grace for the sinner.

When Jesus volunteered to take on Himself the sin of this fallen world to redeem it, He could no longer remain the ruler in the kingdom of glory, for in that kingdom, there is nothing that defiles. Therefore the whole government of heaven was changed in order to redeem this lost world.

The kingdom of grace was instituted immediately after the fall of man, when a plan was devised for the redemption of the guilty race. It then existed in the purpose and by the promise of

God; and through faith, men could become its subjects. Yet it was not actually established until the death of Christ . . . . But when the Saviour yielded up His life, and with His expiring breath cried out, "It is finished," then the fulfillment of the plan of redemption was assured. The promise of salvation made to the sinful pair in Eden was ratified. The kingdom of grace, which had before existed by the promise of God, was then established. (*The Great Controversy*, 347-348)

The kingdom of grace encompasses the whole controversy between Christ and Satan over the unchangeable nature of God's law. In this controversy, Jesus shed His blood on Calvary; therefore, the kingdom of grace is a kingdom of bloodshed. Christ will continue to provide grace to the fallen race through His shed blood until probation closes. His grace and mercy will then be withdrawn from unrepentant sinners. During the closing scenes of the controversy, the kingdom of glory will be restored to its original state, and peace and harmony will once again reign throughout the universe.

To help fallen man understand and keep ever before his mind the great sacrifice that God the Father and His Son Jesus Christ were making to redeem fallen man, the system of sacrifices was introduced.

> The sacrificial offerings were ordained by God to be to man a perpetual reminder and a penitential acknowledgment of his sin and a confession of his faith in the promised Redeemer. They were intended to impress upon the fallen race the solemn truth that it was sin that caused death . . . . A star of hope illumined the dark and terrible future and relieved it of its utter desolation.
>
> But the plan of redemption had a yet broader and deeper purpose than the salvation of man. It was not for this alone that Christ came to the earth; it was not merely that the inhabitants of this little world might regard the law of God as it should be regarded; but it was to vindicate the character of God before the universe. To this result of His great sacrifice—its influence upon the intelligences of other worlds, as well as upon man—the Saviour looked forward when just before His crucifixion He said: "Now is the judgment of this world: now shall the prince of this world be cast out. And I, if I be lifted up from

the earth, will draw all unto Me." John 12:31, 32. The act of Christ in dying for the salvation of man would not only make heaven accessible to men, but before all the universe it would justify God and His Son in their dealing with the rebellion of Satan. It would establish the perpetuity of the law of God and would reveal the nature and the results of sin. (*Patriarchs and Prophets*, 68-69)

3

The Beginning of the Sacrificial System

Heavenly angels more fully opened to our first parents the plan that had been devised for their salvation. Adam and his companion were assured that notwithstanding their great sin, they were not to be abandoned to the control of Satan. The Son of God had offered to atone, with His own life, for their transgression. A period of probation would be granted them, and through repentance and faith in Christ they might again become the children of God.

The sacrifice demanded by their transgression revealed to Adam and Eve the sacred character of the law of God; and they saw, as they had never seen before, the guilt of sin and its dire results. (*Patriarchs and Prophets*, 66)

To Adam, the offering of the first sacrifice was a most painful ceremony. His hand must be raised to take life, which only God could give. It was the first time he had ever witnessed death, and he knew that had he been obedient to God, there would have been no death of man or beast. As he slew the innocent victim, he trembled at the thought that his sin must shed the blood of the spotless Lamb of God. This scene gave him a deeper and more vivid sense of the greatness of his transgression, which nothing but the death of God's dear Son could expiate. And he marveled at the infinite goodness that would give such a ransom to save the guilty. (ibid., 68)

In time, Eve gave birth to two sons. Adam and Eve named the first son *Cain* and the second son *Abel*. As these two sons grew up, Adam and Eve faithfully instructed them in the great plan of redemption. When matured in age, the time came for them to build their own altars and offer their own sacrifices for their sin. The Bible record says,

> Now Abel kept flocks, and Cain worked the soil. In the course of time Cain brought some of the fruits of the soil as an offering to the LORD. But Abel brought fat portions from some of the firstborn of his flock. The LORD looked with favor on Abel and his offering, but on Cain and his offering he did not look with favor. So Cain was very angry, and his face was downcast. Then the LORD said to Cain, "Why are you angry? Why is your face downcast? If you do what is right, will you not be accepted? But if you do not do what is right, sin is crouching at your door; it desires to have you, but you must master it." (Gen. 4:2-7)

> These brothers were tested, as Adam had been tested before them, to prove whether they would believe and obey the word of God. They were acquainted with the provision made for the salvation of man, and understood the system of offerings which God had ordained. They knew that in these offerings they were to express faith in the Saviour whom the offerings typified, and at the same time to acknowledge their total dependence on Him for pardon; and they knew that by thus conforming to the divine plan for their redemption, they were giving proof of their obedience to the will of God. Without the shedding of blood there could be no remission of sin; and they were to show their faith in the blood of Christ as the promised atonement by offering the firstlings of the flock in sacrifice. (ibid., 71)

> Cain came before God with murmuring and infidelity in his heart in regard to the promised sacrifice and the necessity of the sacrificial offerings. His gift expressed no penitence for sin. He felt, as many now feel, that it would be an acknowledgment of weakness to follow the exact plan marked out by God, of trusting his salvation wholly to the atonement of the promised Saviour. He chose the course of self-dependence. He would come in his own merits. He would not bring the lamb, and mingle its blood with his offering, but would present his fruits, the products of his labor. He presented his offering as a favor done to God, through

which he expected to secure the divine approval. Cain obeyed in building an altar, obeyed in bringing a sacrifice; but he rendered only a partial obedience. The essential part, the recognition of the need of a Redeemer, was left out. (ibid., 72)

"By faith Abel offered unto God a more excellent sacrifice than Cain." Hebrews 11:4. Abel grasped the great principles of redemption. He saw himself a sinner, and he saw sin and its penalty, death, standing between his soul and communion with God. He brought the slain victim, the sacrificed life, thus acknowledging the claims of the law that had been transgressed. Through the shed blood he looked to the future sacrifice, Christ dying on the cross of Calvary; and trusting in the atonement that was there to be made, he had the witness that he was righteous, and his offering accepted. (ibid.)

Abel chose faith and obedience; Cain, unbelief and rebellion. Here the whole matter rested.

Cain and Abel represent two classes that will exist in the world till the close of time. (ibid.)

Altars were built, and sacrifices were offered by all the faithful patriarchal families to the time of the flood. Adam instructed Enoch in the purpose of these sacrifices. Enoch taught his son Methuselah, who lived 600 years with Noah, concerning the purpose of the sacrifices. But the majority of the people rebelled against God.

The period of their probation was about to expire. Noah had faithfully followed the instructions which he had received from God. The ark was finished in every part as the Lord had directed, and was stored with food for man and beast . . . .

God commanded Noah, "Come thou and all thy house into the ark; for thee have I seen righteous before Me in this generation." Noah's warnings had been rejected by the world, but his influence and example resulted in blessings to his family. As a reward for his faithfulness and integrity, God saved all the members of his family with him. (ibid., 97-98)

So God sent a flood upon the earth and destroyed mankind except for Noah and his family.

Noah and his family anxiously waited for the decrease
of the waters, for they longed to go forth again upon the
earth. . . .

At last an angel descended from heaven, opened the
massive door, and bade the patriarch and his household go forth
upon the earth and take with them every living thing. In the joy
of their release Noah did not forget Him by whose gracious
care they had been preserved. His first act after leaving the
ark was to build an altar and offer from every kind of clean
beast and fowl a sacrifice, thus manifesting his gratitude to
God for deliverance and his faith in Christ, the great sacrifice.
(ibid., 105-106)

In Genesis, we read that "Noah came out, together with his sons and
his wife and his sons' wives." "Then Noah built an altar to the LORD and,
taking some of all the clean animals and clean birds, he sacrificed burnt
offerings on it." "Then God blessed Noah and his sons, saying to them, 'Be
fruitful and increase in number and fill the earth.'" (Gen. 8:18, 20, 9:1)

Abraham, who was born only eight years after Noah died, learned of
the meaning of the sacrifices from Noah's son, Shem. Thus through the
sacrificial system, the faith of the patriarchs in Jesus as the Lamb of God
was preserved from generation to generation.

It was to impress Abraham's mind with the reality of the
gospel, as well as to test his faith, that God commanded him to
slay his son. The agony which he endured during the dark days
of that fearful trial was permitted that he might understand from
his own experience something of the greatness of the sacrifice
made by the infinite God for man's redemption. No other test
could have caused Abraham such torture of soul as did the
offering of his son. God gave His Son to a death of agony and
shame. The angels who witnessed the humiliation and soul
anguish of the Son of God were not permitted to interpose, as
in the case of Isaac. There was no voice to cry, "It is enough."
To save the fallen race, the King of glory yielded up His life.
What stronger proof can be given of the infinite compassion and
love of God? "He that spared not His own Son, but delivered
Him up for us all, how shall He not with Him also freely give
us all things?" Romans 8:32.

The sacrifice required of Abraham was not alone for his own good, nor solely for the benefit of succeeding generations; but it was also for the instruction of the sinless intelligences of heaven and of other worlds. The field of the controversy between Christ and Satan—the field on which the plan of redemption is wrought out—is the lesson book of the universe. (ibid., 154)

It had been difficult even for the angels to grasp the mystery of redemption—to comprehend that the Commander of heaven, the Son of God, must die for guilty man. When the command was given to Abraham to offer up his son, the interest of all heavenly beings was enlisted. With intense earnestness they watched each step in the fulfillment of this command. When to Isaac's question, "Where is the lamb for a burnt offering?" Abraham made answer, "God will provide Himself a lamb;" and when the father's hand was stayed as he was about to slay his son, and the ram which God had provided was offered in the place of Isaac—then light was shed upon the mystery of redemption, and even the angels understood more clearly the wonderful provision that God had made for man's salvation. 1 Peter 1:12. (ibid., 155)

4

A Sanctuary for the Lamb

Isaac understood that he was a representative of Christ, the Lamb of God slain from the foundation of the world. Faithfully did Isaac and Rebekah instruct their boys concerning the promise of the Redeemer demonstrated by the sacrificial system.

> The promises made to Abraham and confirmed to his son were held by Isaac and Rebekah as the great object of their desires and hopes. With these promises Esau and Jacob were familiar. They were taught to regard the birthright as a matter of great importance, for it included not only an inheritance of worldly wealth, but spiritual pre-eminence. He who received it was to be the priest of his family, and in the line of his posterity the Redeemer of the world would come. On the other hand, there were obligations resting upon the possessor of the birthright. He who should inherit its blessings must devote his life to the service of God. Like Abraham, he must be obedient to the divine requirements. In marriage, in his family relations, in public life, he must consult the will of God.
>
> Isaac made known to his sons these privileges and conditions. (*Patriarchs and Prophets*, 177-178)

Before Jacob left his father's house to flee from the wrath of Esau, Isaac reminded him of the promises made to Abraham.

> May God Almighty bless you and make you fruitful and increase your numbers until you become a community of peoples. May he give you and your descendants the blessing given to Abraham, so that you may take possession of the land

where you now live as an alien, the land God gave to Abraham. (Gen. 28:3-4)

God Himself renewed the promises to Jacob on his way to Laban's home.

> There above it [the ladder] stood the LORD, and he said: "I am the LORD, the God of your father Abraham and the God of Isaac. I will give you and your descendants the land on which you are lying . . . . All peoples on earth will be blessed through you and your offspring." (Gen. 28:13-14)
>
> With deep gratitude he [Jacob] repeated the promise that God's presence would be with him; and then he made the solemn vow, "If God will be with me, and will keep me in this way that I go, and will give me bread to eat, and raiment to put on, so that I come again to my father's house in peace; then shall the Lord be my God: and this stone, which I have set for a pillar, shall be God's house: and of all that Thou shalt give me I will surely give the tenth unto Thee."
>
> Jacob was not here seeking to make terms with God. The Lord had already promised him prosperity, and this vow was the outflow of a heart filled with gratitude for the assurance of God's love and mercy. Jacob felt that God had claims upon him which he must acknowledge, and that the special tokens of divine favor granted him demanded a return. (ibid., 187)

From Adam to Jacob, we have seen that the altar with the lamb sacrifice was the central theme of the patriarchal economy. These men of God saw that with these sacrifices was bound up the promise of God to provide for them a Redeemer.

Near the end of his long life, a widespread famine occurred in the land, and Jacob moved his family to Egypt where they were provided with food during this crisis. At first, they were received with favor in Egypt and lived in freedom. But after some years passed, a new king came to the throne that did not look with favor on the Hebrew people. He began to oppress them and after a time subjected the Israelites to bondage and slavery. Under these oppressive conditions, the people began to let their interest in the sacrificial system wane, and their faith in the promised Redeemer grew dim.

When the Lord brought Israel out of Egypt, they were more like a small nation in number than a patriarchal family. At this time, God replaced the family altar with the sanctuary and its attendant services. The Lord instructed them saying, "Then have them make a sanctuary for me, and I will dwell among them" (Exod. 25:8). God loved them, and He desired to dwell among them. He desired to teach them about Jesus, the Lamb of God, who would give His life to cover their sin. The Lord also wanted to dwell among them so He could protect them from the attacks of Satan who was bent on their destruction.

The sanctuary was located right in the center of their encampment with three of the tribes located on each of the four sides.

> The tabernacle was so constructed that it could be removed from place to place; yet it was a structure of great magnificence. Its walls consisted of upright boards heavily plated with gold and set in sockets of silver, while the roof was formed of a series of curtains, or coverings, the outer of skins, the innermost of fine linen beautifully wrought with figures of cherubim. Besides the outer court, which contained the altar of burnt offering, the tabernacle itself consisted of two apartments called the holy and the most holy place, separated by a rich and beautiful curtain, or veil; a similar veil closed the entrance to the first apartment.
>
> In the holy place was the candlestick, on the south, with its seven lamps giving light to the sanctuary both by day and by night; on the north stood the table of shewbread; and before the veil separating the holy from the most holy was the golden altar of incense, from which the cloud of fragrance, with the prayers of Israel, was daily ascending before God.
>
> In the most holy place stood the ark, a chest of precious wood overlaid with gold, the depository of the two tables of stone upon which God had inscribed the law of Ten Commandments. Above the ark, and forming the cover to the sacred chest, was the mercy seat, a magnificent piece of workmanship, surmounted by two cherubim, one at each end, and all wrought of solid gold. In this apartment the divine presence was manifested in the cloud of glory between the cherubim. (*The Great Controversy*, 412)
>
> The ministration of the earthly sanctuary consisted of two divisions; the priests ministered daily in the holy place,

while once a year the high priest performed a special work of atonement in the most holy, for the cleansing of the sanctuary. Day by day the repentant sinner brought his offering to the door of the tabernacle and, placing his hand upon the victim's head, confessed his sins, thus in figure transferring them from himself to the innocent sacrifice. The animal was then slain. "Without shedding of blood," says the apostle, there is no remission of sin. [Hebrews 9:22.] "The life of the flesh is in the blood." Leviticus 17:11. The broken law of God demanded the life of the transgressor. The blood, representing the forfeited life of the sinner, whose guilt the victim bore, was carried by the priest into the holy place and sprinkled before the veil, behind which was the ark containing the law that the sinner had transgressed. By this ceremony the sin was, through the blood, transferred in figure to the sanctuary . . . .

Such was the work that went on, day by day, throughout the year. The sins of Israel were thus transferred to the sanctuary, and a special work became necessary for their removal. (ibid., 418)

Once a year, on the great Day of Atonement, the priest entered the most holy place for the cleansing of the sanctuary. The work there performed completed the yearly round of ministration. On the Day of Atonement, two kids of the goats were brought to the door of the tabernacle, and lots were cast upon them, "one lot for the Lord, and the other lot for the scapegoat." [Leviticus 16] Verse 8. The goat upon which fell the lot for the Lord was to be slain as a sin offering for the people. And the priest was to bring his blood within the veil and sprinkle it upon the mercy seat and before the mercy seat. The blood was also to be sprinkled upon the altar of incense that was before the veil.

"And Aaron shall lay both his hands upon the head of the live goat, and confess over him all the iniquities of the children of Israel, and all their transgressions in all their sins, putting them upon the head of the goat, and shall send him away by the hand of a fit man into the wilderness: and the goat shall bear upon him all their iniquities unto a land not inhabited." [Leviticus 16] Verses 21, 22. The scapegoat came no more into the camp of Israel, and the man who led him away was required to wash himself and his clothing with water before returning to the camp.

The whole ceremony was designed to impress the Israelites with the holiness of God and His abhorrence of sin; and, further, to show them that they could not come in contact with sin without becoming polluted. Every man was required to afflict his soul while this work of atonement was going forward. All business was to be laid aside, and the whole congregation of Israel were to spend the day in solemn humiliation before God, with prayer, fasting, and deep searching of heart.

Important truths concerning the atonement are taught by the typical service. A substitute was accepted in the sinner's stead; but the sin was not canceled by the blood of the victim. A means was thus provided by which it was transferred to the sanctuary. By the offering of blood the sinner acknowledged the authority of the law, confessed his guilt in transgression, and expressed his desire for pardon through faith in a Redeemer to come; but he was not yet entirely released from the condemnation of the law. On the Day of Atonement the high priest, having taken an offering from the congregation, went into the most holy place with the blood of this offering, and sprinkled it upon the mercy seat, directly over the law, to make satisfaction for its claims. Then, in his character of mediator, he took the sins upon himself and bore them from the sanctuary. Placing his hands upon the head of the scapegoat, he confessed over him all these sins, thus in figure transferring them from himself to the goat. The goat then bore them away, and they were regarded as forever separated from the people. (ibid., 419-420)

As the altar with the lamb sacrifice was the central focus of the patriarchal family from Adam to Jacob, so now the sanctuary and its services became the focal point of the whole Jewish economy from the time of the Exodus to the death of Jesus on the cross.

The Old Testament Sanctuary and Courtyard

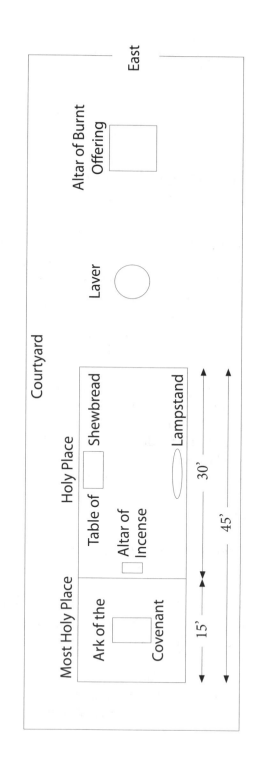

5

The History of the Sanctuary on Earth

The exodus of the children of Israel from their slavery in Egypt took place in 1445 BC. God led the people into the wilderness to a place called Mount Sinai, where they set up camp. Soon after they were settled, the Lord called Moses up on the mountain.

> When Moses went up on the mountain, the cloud covered it, and the glory of the LORD settled on Mount Sinai. (Exod. 24:15-16)
>
> Then Moses entered the cloud as he went on up the mountain. And he stayed on the mountain forty days and forty nights. (Exod. 24:18)
>
> The LORD said to Moses, "Tell the Israelites to bring me an offering. You are to receive the offering for me from each man whose heart prompts him to give." "Then have them make a sanctuary for me, and I will dwell among them." (Exod. 25:1-2, 8)

The construction of the sanctuary continued for about half a year. It "was set up on the first day of the first month in the second year" (Exod. 40:17). This was in 1443 BC.

As the children of Israel wandered in the wilderness the next thirty-eight years, they moved the tabernacle to each new encampment. When they entered the Promised Land, the sanctuary was permanently set up at Shiloh.

During His reign as king, David began to lay plans for the construction of a temple in Jerusalem in which to house the sanctuary services. The God of heaven intervened in David's plans and only allowed him to assemble the materials. The actual construction of the temple was deferred to his son Solomon.

> In the four hundred and eightieth year after the Israelites had come out of Egypt, in the fourth year of Solomon's reign over Israel, in the month of Ziv, the second month, he began to build the temple of the LORD. (1 Kings 6:1)

The year was 966 BC. "The foundation of the temple of the LORD was laid in the fourth year, in the month of Ziv. In the eleventh year in the month of Bul, the eighth month, the temple was finished in all its details according to its specifications. He had spent seven years building it." (1 Kings 6:37-38)

Thus the temple built by Solomon was dedicated in 959 BC. The sanctuary services were housed in the tent of meeting for 484 years. See chart at the end of this chapter.

The people of Israel came to this temple for nearly five centuries to offer their sacrifices and to worship. But when King Zedekiah of Judah rebelled against the king of Babylon, the Babylonian army came and laid siege to the city of Jerusalem. In the attack, the city was destroyed and the temple burned down.

> On the seventh day of the fifth month, in the nineteenth year of Nebuchadnezzar king of Babylon, Nebuzaradan commander of the imperial guard, an official of the king of Babylon, came to Jerusalem. He set fire to the temple of the LORD, the royal palace and all the houses of Jerusalem. Every important building he burned down. (2 Kings 25:8-9)

The year was 586 BC; therefore, the temple built by Solomon had a life span of 373 years.

When Cyrus, king of Medo-Persia, captured the nation of Babylon, he gave the Jews permission to return to Jerusalem and rebuild the temple. This decree, recorded in Ezra 1, was issued in 539 BC, but this effort ended in failure. In 520 BC, another decree was issued, this one by Darius. This second decree is recorded in Ezra 6. This time the rebuilding of the temple was successfully completed, and it was dedicated in 516 BC. Thus the temple lay in ruins for seventy years.

> Then, because of the decree King Darius had sent, Tattenai, governor of Trans-Euphrates, and Shethar-Bozenai and their associates carried it out with diligence. So the elders of the Jews continued to build and prosper under the preaching of Haggai the prophet and Zechariah, a descendant of Iddo. They finished building the temple according to the command of the God of Israel. The temple was completed on the third day of the month Adar, in the sixth year of the reign of King Darius.
>
> Then the people of Israel—the priests, the Levites and the rest of the exiles—celebrated the dedication of the house of God with joy. For the dedication of this house of God they offered a hundred bulls, two hundred rams, four hundred male lambs and, as a sin offering for all Israel, twelve male goats, one for each of the tribes of Israel. And they installed the priests in their divisions and the Levites in their groups for the service of God at Jerusalem, according to what is written in the Book of Moses. (Ezra 6:13-18)

The Jews knew that it was because of their apostasy and sin that the temple was destroyed, and they were sent into captivity for these seventy years. They were very grateful that the Lord again looked with favor upon them and gave them the privilege to reestablish the sacrificial services. They renewed their faith in the promise of a Redeemer who would come to shed His blood to pay the price for their sin.

> The second temple did not equal the first in magnificence, nor was it hallowed by those visible tokens of the divine presence which pertained to the first temple. There was no manifestation of supernatural power to mark its dedication. No cloud of glory was seen to fill the newly erected sanctuary. No fire from heaven descended to consume the sacrifice upon its altar. The Shekinah no longer abode between the cherubim in the most holy place; the ark, the mercy seat, and the tables of testimony were not found there. No sign from heaven made known to the inquiring priest the will of Jehovah.
>
> And yet this was the building concerning which the Lord had declared by the prophet Haggai: "The glory of this latter

house shall be greater than of the former." "I will shake all nations, and the Desire of all nations shall come: and I will fill this house with glory, saith the Lord of hosts." Haggai 2:9, 7. For centuries learned men have endeavored to show wherein the promise of God, given to Haggai, has been fulfilled; yet in the advent of Jesus of Nazareth, the Desire of all nations, who by His personal presence hallowed the precincts of the temple, many have steadfastly refused to see any special significance. Pride and unbelief have blinded their minds to the true meaning of the prophet's words.

The second temple was honored, not with the cloud of Jehovah's glory, but with the presence of the One in whom dwelt "all the fullness of the Godhead bodily"—God Himself "manifest in the flesh." Colossians 2:9; 1 Timothy 3:16. In being honored with the personal presence of Christ during His earthly ministry, and in this alone, did the second temple exceed the first in glory. The "Desire of all nations" had indeed come to His temple, when the Man of Nazareth taught and healed in the sacred courts. (*Prophets and Kings*, 596-597)

Some 545 years later, the long-awaited Messiah came, but they did not recognize Him.

"I baptize with water," John replied, "but among you stands one you do not know. He is the one who comes after me, the thongs of whose sandals I am not worthy to untie." This all happened at Bethany on the other side of the Jordan, where John was baptizing.

The next day John saw Jesus coming toward him and said, "Look, the Lamb of God, who takes away the sin of the world! This is the one I meant when I said, 'A man who comes after me has surpassed me because he was before me.' I myself did not know him, but the reason I came baptizing with water was that he might be revealed to Israel."

Then John gave this testimony: "I saw the Spirit come down from heaven as a dove and remain on him. I would not have known him, except that the one who sent me to baptize with water told me, 'The man on whom you see the Spirit come down and remain is he who will baptize with the Holy Spirit.' I have seen and I testify that this is the Son of God." (John 1:26-34)

For four thousand years, the faithful people of God had sacrificed a lamb morning and evening, expressing their faith in the promised Lamb of God to come. But when He came and John pointed Him out to them, they would not recognize Him or accept Him. Three and one half years later, they crucified Him as a malefactor.

> When they came to the place called the Skull, there they crucified him, along with the criminals—one on his right, the other on his left. Jesus said, "Father, forgive them, for they do not know what they are doing." (Luke 23:33-34)
>
> And when Jesus had cried out again in a loud voice, he gave up his spirit. At that moment the curtain of the temple was torn in two from top to bottom. (Matt. 27:50-51)
>
> When the loud cry, "It is finished," came from the lips of Christ, the priests were officiating in the temple. It was the hour of the evening sacrifice. The lamb representing Christ had been brought to be slain. Clothed in his significant and beautiful dress, the priest stood with lifted knife, as did Abraham when he was about to slay his son. With intense interest the people were looking on. But the earth trembles and quakes; for the Lord Himself draws near. With a rending noise the inner veil of the temple is torn from top to bottom by an unseen hand, throwing open to the gaze of the multitude a place once filled with the presence of God. In this place the Shekinah had dwelt. Here God had manifested His glory above the mercy seat. No one but the high priest ever lifted the veil separating this apartment from the rest of the temple. He entered in once a year to make an atonement for the sins of the people. But lo, this veil is rent in twain. The most holy place of the earthly sanctuary is no longer sacred.
>
> All is terror and confusion. The priest is about to slay the victim; but the knife drops from his nerveless hand, and the lamb escapes. Type has met antitype in the death of God's Son. The great sacrifice has been made. The way into the holiest is laid open. A new and living way is prepared for all. No longer need sinful, sorrowing humanity await the coming

of the high priest. Henceforth the Saviour was to officiate as priest and advocate in the heaven of heavens. It was as if a living voice had spoken to the worshipers: There is now an end to all sacrifices and offerings for sin. The Son of God is come according to His word, "Lo, I come (in the volume of the Book it is written of Me,) to do Thy will, O God." "By His own blood" He entereth "in once into the holy place, having obtained eternal redemption for us." Hebrews 10:7; 9:12. (*The Desire of Ages*, 756-757)

Because the Jews rejected the Lamb of God, the following curse was uttered a few days before He was crucified:

Jesus left the temple and was walking away when his disciples came up to him to call his attention to its buildings. "Do you see all these things?" he asked. "I tell you the truth, not one stone here will be left on another; every one will be thrown down." (Matt. 24:1-2)

Thus the Jewish leaders had built up "Zion with blood, and Jerusalem with iniquity." Micah 3:10. And yet, while they slew their Saviour because He reproved their sins, such was their self-righteousness that they regarded themselves as God's favored people and expected the Lord to deliver them from their enemies. "Therefore," continued the prophet, "shall Zion for your sake be plowed as a field, and Jerusalem shall become heaps, and the mountain of the house as the high places of the forest." Verse 12.

For nearly forty years after the doom of Jerusalem had been pronounced by Christ Himself, the Lord delayed His judgments upon the city and the nation. Wonderful was the long-suffering of God toward the rejectors of His gospel and the murderers of His Son. (*The Great Controversy*, 27)

This prophecy was fulfilled literally in AD 70 when the Romans, under Titus, completely destroyed Jerusalem and the temple buildings. When this temple was destroyed, it was never replaced. There has not been a sanctuary on earth since that time in which the sacrificial services have been conducted. This is important to keep in mind as we study the prophecies regarding the time of the end.

History of the Sanctuary on Earth

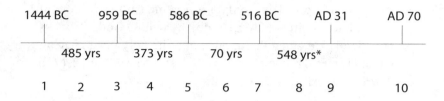

1. Sanctuary built by Israel at Mt. Sinai
2. Sanctuary service housed in a tent
3. Temple built by Solomon
4. Sanctuary services conducted in the temple built by Solomon
5. Temple destroyed by Nebuchadnezzar
6. Sanctuary lay in ruins
7. Temple rebuilt—dedicated by Haggai, Zechariah and Ezra
8. Sanctuary services conducted in this temple until the death of Jesus
9. Veil torn when Jesus died on the cross and thus ended the sacrificial service on earth
10. Temple destroyed (it has never been rebuilt, and the sacrificial system has never been reinstated in Jerusalem)

   * When moving from BC to AD, one year needs to be added to account for the "0" year

6

The Two Sanctuaries

In the previous chapter, we reviewed the history of the sanctuary on earth.

> This is the only sanctuary that ever existed on the earth, of which the Bible gives any information. This was declared by Paul to be the sanctuary of the first covenant. But has the new covenant no sanctuary? (*The Great Controversy*, 412-413)
>
> The holy places made with hands were to be "figures of the true," "patterns of things in the heavens" (Hebrews 9:24, 23)—a miniature representation of the heavenly temple where Christ, our great High Priest, after offering His life as a sacrifice, was to minister in the sinner's behalf. God presented before Moses in the mount a view of the heavenly sanctuary, and commanded him to make all things according to the pattern shown him. (*Patriarchs and Prophets*, 343)
>
> Turning again to the book of Hebrews, the seekers for truth found that the existence of a second, or new-covenant sanctuary, was implied in the words of Paul already quoted: "Then verily the first covenant had also ordinances of divine service, and a worldly sanctuary." And the use of the word "also" intimates that Paul has before made mention of this sanctuary. Turning back to the beginning of the previous chapter, they read: "Now of the things which we have spoken this is the sum: We have such an High Priest, who is set on the right hand of the throne of the Majesty in the heavens; a Minister of the sanctuary, and of the true tabernacle, which the Lord pitched, and not man." Hebrews 8:1, 2.

Here is revealed the sanctuary of the new covenant. The
sanctuary of the first covenant was pitched by man, built by
Moses; this is pitched by the Lord, not by man. In that sanctuary
the earthly priests performed their service; in this, Christ, our
great High Priest, ministers at God's right hand. One sanctuary
was on earth, the other is in heaven.

Further, the tabernacle built by Moses was made after a
pattern. The Lord directed him: "According to all that I show
thee, after the pattern of the tabernacle, and the pattern of all
the instruments thereof, even so shall ye make it." And again
the charge was given, "Look that thou make them after their
pattern, which was showed thee in the mount." Exodus 25:9,
40. (*The Great Controversy*, 413)

The lampstand was to be made exactly like the pattern shown him
in the mount.

This is how the lampstand was made: It was made of hammered
gold—from its base to its blossoms. The lampstand was made
exactly like the pattern the LORD had shown Moses. (Num. 8:4)

The altar of burnt offering was also "made just as you were shown
on the mountain" (Exod. 27:8).

Even the setting up of the tabernacle was "according to the plan shown
you on the mountain" (Exod. 26:30).

And Paul says that the first tabernacle "was a figure for
the time then present, in which were offered both gifts and
sacrifices;" that its holy places were "patterns of things in the
heavens;" that the priests who offered gifts according to the
law served "unto the example and shadow of heavenly things,"
and that "Christ is not entered into the holy places made with
hands, which are the figures of the true; but into heaven itself,
now to appear in the presence of God for us." Hebrews 9:9, 23;
8:5; 9:24. (ibid., 413)

When it was completed, Moses examined all the work of
the builders, comparing it with the pattern shown him in the
mount and the directions he had received from God. "As the
Lord had commanded, even so had they done it: and Moses

blessed them." With eager interest the multitudes of Israel crowded around to look upon the sacred structure. (*Patriarchs and Prophets*, 349)

The sanctuary in heaven, in which Jesus ministers in our behalf, is the great original, of which the sanctuary built by Moses was a copy. (*The Great Controversy*, 414)

The subject of the sanctuary and the investigative judgment should be clearly understood by the people of God. All need a knowledge for themselves of the position and work of their great High Priest. Otherwise it will be *impossible* for them to exercise the faith which is essential at this time or to occupy the position which God designs them to fill. Every individual has a soul to save or to lose. Each has a case pending at the bar of God. Each must meet the great Judge face to face . . . .

All who have received the light upon these subjects are to bear testimony of the great truths which God has committed to them. *The sanctuary in heaven is the very center of Christ's work in behalf of men. It concerns every soul living upon the earth.* It opens to view the plan of redemption, bringing us down to the very close of time and revealing the triumphant issue of the contest between righteousness and sin. It is of the utmost importance that all should thoroughly investigate these subjects and be able to give an answer to everyone that asketh them a reason of the hope that is in them.

The intercession of Christ in man's behalf in the sanctuary above is as essential to the plan of salvation as was His death upon the cross. By His death He began that work which after His resurrection He ascended to complete in heaven. We must by faith enter within the veil, "whither the forerunner is for us entered." Hebrews 6:20. There the light from the cross of Calvary is reflected. There we may gain a clearer insight into the mysteries of redemption. The salvation of man is accomplished at an infinite expense to heaven; the sacrifice made is equal to the broadest demands of the broken law of God. Jesus has opened the way to the Father's throne, and through His mediation the sincere desire of all who come to Him in faith may be presented before God. (ibid., 488-489) (Emphasis supplied.)

7

The Lamb Opens the Holy Place

Forty days after Jesus was raised from the dead, He and His disciples were walking toward Bethany. When they reached the crest of the Mount of Olives, "he lifted up his hands and blessed them. While he was blessing them, he left them and was taken up into heaven." "He was taken up before their very eyes, and a cloud hid him from their sight." (Luke 24:50-51; Acts 1:9)

Many years later when John was on the Isle of Patmos, he was shown in vision the arrival of Jesus in heaven after His ascension.

Beginning with Revelation 4:1, John gives a detailed description of the setting in which Jesus appeared. Struggling to find words to adequately describe the glories of the scene before him, he writes,

> After this I looked, and there before me was a door standing open in heaven. And the voice I had first heard speaking to me like a trumpet said, "Come up here, and I will show you what must take place after this." At once I was in the Spirit, and there before me was a throne in heaven with someone sitting on it. And the one who sat there had the appearance of jasper and carnelian. A rainbow, resembling an emerald, encircled the throne. (Rev. 4:1-3)

Who was sitting on this throne before which the "Lamb, looking as if it had been slain" (Rev. 5:6), was standing? It is God the Father, the Ancient of Days, the great ruler of the universe. He is the One who "so loved the world, that he gave his only begotten Son, that whosoever believeth in him should not perish, but have everlasting life" (John 3:16, KJV). This is the One before whom the Lamb is standing.

Surrounding the throne were twenty-four other thrones, and seated on them were twenty-four elders. They were dressed in white and had crowns of gold on their heads. From the throne came flashes of lightning, rumblings and peals of thunder. Before the throne, seven lamps were blazing. (Rev. 4:4-5)

As in vision the apostle John was granted a view of the temple of God in heaven, he beheld there "seven lamps of fire burning before the throne." Revelation 4:5. He saw an angel "having a golden censer; and there was given unto him much incense, that he should offer it with the prayers of all saints upon the golden altar which was before the throne." Revelation 8:3. Here the prophet was permitted to behold the first apartment of the sanctuary in heaven; and he saw there the "seven lamps of fire" and "the golden altar," represented by the golden candlestick and the altar of incense in the sanctuary on earth. (*The Great Controversy*, 414-415)

In the sanctuary on earth, the lampstand was located in the first apartment. So we see that Revelation 4 is a description of the scene taking place in the holy place of the sanctuary in heaven at the time Jesus ascended from this earth.

Also before the throne there was what looked like a sea of glass, clear as crystal.

In the center, around the throne, were four living creatures, and they were covered with eyes, in front and in back . . . . Day and night they never stop saying: "Holy, holy, holy is the Lord God Almighty, who was, and is, and is to come." Whenever the living creatures give glory, honor and thanks to him who sits on the throne and who lives for ever and ever, the twenty-four elders fall down before him who sits on the throne, and worship him who lives for ever and ever. They lay their crowns before the throne and say: "You are worthy, our Lord and God, to receive glory and honor and power, for you created all things, and by your will they were created and have their being." (Rev. 4:6-11)

In the midst of this glorious celebration, John describes the appearance of Jesus as He comes before the Father.

> Then, midway between the throne and the four living
> creatures, I saw a Lamb standing among the Elders. He looked
> as if He had been offered in sacrifice. (Rev. 5:6, WNT)

In Revelation 4 and 5, John is describing the vastness and glory
of the sanctuary in heaven and the inauguration of Jesus as our high
priest.

> The matchless splendor of the earthly tabernacle reflected
> to human vision the glories of that heavenly temple where Christ
> our forerunner ministers for us before the throne of God. The
> abiding place of the King of kings, where thousand thousands
> minister unto Him, and ten thousand times ten thousand stand
> before Him (Daniel 7:10); that temple, filled with the glory of
> the eternal throne, where seraphim, its shining guardians, veil
> their faces in adoration, could find, in the most magnificent
> structure ever reared by human hands, but a faint reflection of
> its vastness and glory. (ibid., 414)

Ever since this celebration of the opening of the holy place in the
sanctuary in heaven, Christ, the Lamb slain from the foundation of the
world, has been ministering His blood for the remission of our sins in
this sacred place.

> The point of what we are saying is this: We do have such a
> high priest, who sat down at the right hand of the throne of the
> Majesty in heaven, and who serves in the sanctuary, the true
> tabernacle set up by the Lord, not by man. (Heb. 8:1-2)

The following is another description of this same event as recorded
in *The Desire of Ages* (833-835).

> All heaven was waiting to welcome the Saviour to the
> celestial courts. As He ascended, He led the way, and the
> multitude of captives set free at His resurrection followed.
> The heavenly host, with shouts and acclamations of praise and
> celestial song, attended the joyous train.
>   As they drew near to the city of God, the challenge is given
> by the escorting angels,—

"Lift up your heads, O ye gates;
And be ye lift up, ye everlasting doors;
And the King of glory shall come in."

Joyfully the waiting sentinels respond,—

"Who is this King of glory?"

This they say, not because they know not who He is, but because they would hear the answer of exalted praise,—

"The Lord strong and mighty,
The Lord mighty in battle!
Lift up your heads, O ye gates;
Even lift them up, ye everlasting doors;
And the King of glory shall come in."

Again is heard the challenge, "Who is this King of glory?" for the angels never weary of hearing His name exalted. The escorting angels make reply,—

"The Lord of hosts;
He is the King of glory." (Ps. 24:7-10)

Then the portals of the city of God are opened wide, and the angelic throng sweep through the gates amid a burst of rapturous music.

There is the throne, and around it the rainbow of promise. There are cherubim and seraphim. The commanders of the angel hosts, the sons of God, the representatives of the unfallen worlds, are assembled. The heavenly council before which Lucifer had accused God and His Son, the representatives of those sinless realms over which Satan had thought to establish his dominion,—all are there to welcome the Redeemer. They are eager to celebrate His triumph and to glorify their King.

But He waves them back. Not yet; He cannot now receive the coronet of glory and the royal robe. He enters into the presence of His Father. He points to His wounded head, the pierced side, the marred feet; He lifts His hands, bearing the print of nails. He points to the tokens of His triumph; He presents to God the wave sheaf, those raised with Him as representatives of that great multitude who shall come forth from the grave at His second coming. He approaches the Father, with whom there is joy over one sinner that repents; who rejoices over one with singing. Before the foundations of the earth were laid, the Father and the Son had united in a covenant to redeem man if he should be overcome by Satan. They had clasped Their hands in a solemn pledge that Christ should become the surety for the human race. This pledge Christ has fulfilled. When upon the cross He cried out, "It is finished," He addressed the Father. The compact had been fully carried out. Now He declares: Father, it is finished. I have done Thy will, O My God. I have completed the work of redemption. If Thy justice is satisfied, "I will that they also, whom Thou hast given Me, be with Me where I am." John 19:30; 17:24.

The voice of God is heard proclaiming that justice is satisfied. Satan is vanquished. Christ's toiling, struggling ones on earth are "accepted in the Beloved." Eph. 1:6. Before the heavenly angels and the representatives of unfallen worlds, they are declared justified. Where He is, there His church shall be. "Mercy and truth are met together; righteousness and peace have kissed each other." Ps. 85:10. The Father's arms encircle His Son, and the word is given, "Let all the angels of God worship Him." Heb. 1:6.

With joy unutterable, rulers and principalities and powers acknowledge the supremacy of the Prince of life. The angel host prostrate themselves before Him, while the glad shout fills all the courts of heaven, "Worthy is the Lamb that was slain to receive power, and riches, and wisdom, and strength, and honor, and glory, and blessing." Rev. 5:12.

Songs of triumph mingle with the music from angel harps, till heaven seems to overflow with joy and praise. Love has conquered. The lost is found. Heaven rings with voices in lofty strains proclaiming, "Blessing, and honor, and glory, and power, be unto Him that sitteth upon the throne, and unto the Lamb forever and ever." Rev. 5:13.

From that scene of heavenly joy, there comes back to us on earth the echo of Christ's own wonderful words, "I ascend unto

My Father, and your Father; and to My God, and your God."
John 20:17. The family of heaven and the family of earth are
one. For us our Lord ascended, and for us He lives. "Wherefore
He is able also to save them to the uttermost that come unto
God by Him, seeing He ever liveth to make intercession for
them." Heb. 7:25.

8

The Dragon Pursues the Woman

Satanic agencies confederated with evil men in leading the people to believe Christ the chief of sinners, and to make Him the object of detestation. Those who mocked Christ as He hung upon the cross were imbued with the spirit of the first great rebel. He filled them with vile and loathsome speeches. He inspired their taunts. But by all this he gained nothing.

Could one sin have been found in Christ, had He in one particular yielded to Satan to escape the terrible torture, the enemy of God and man would have triumphed. Christ bowed His head and died, but He held fast His faith and His submission to God. "And I heard a loud voice saying in heaven, Now is come salvation, and strength, and the kingdom of our God, and the power of His Christ: for the accuser of our brethren is cast down, which accused them before our God day and night." Rev. 12:10.

Satan saw that his disguise was torn away. His administration was laid open before the unfallen angels and before the heavenly universe. He had revealed himself as a murderer. By shedding the blood of the Son of God, he had uprooted himself from the sympathies of the heavenly beings. Henceforth his work was restricted. Whatever attitude he might assume, he could no longer await the angels as they came from the heavenly courts, and before them accuse Christ's brethren of being clothed with the garments of blackness and the defilement of sin. The last link of sympathy between Satan and the heavenly world was broken. (*The Desire of Ages*, 760-761)

"When the dragon saw that he had been hurled to the earth, he pursued the woman who had given birth to the male child." "The woman fled into the desert to a place prepared for her by God, where she might be taken care of for 1,260 days"—"a time, times and half a time, out of the serpent's reach." (Rev. 12:13, 6, 14)

Who was this woman (church) that Satan pursued into the wilderness for 1,260 years? Soon after Jesus opened His public ministry He "went up on a mountainside and called to him those he wanted, and they came to him. He appointed twelve—designating them apostles—that they might be with him and that he might send them out to preach." (Mark 3:13-14)

> The first step was now to be taken in the organization of the church that after Christ's departure was to be His representative on earth. (ibid., 291)

At the close of His ministry on earth, Jesus gave His life on the cross. Through His shed blood, He gained authority to "rule all the nations with an iron scepter" (Rev. 12:5). With this authority, Jesus commissioned His disciples saying,

> All authority in heaven and on earth has been given to me. Therefore go and make disciples of all nations, baptizing them in the name of the Father and of the Son and of the Holy Spirit, and teaching them to obey everything I have commanded you. And surely I am with you always, to the very end of the age. (Matt. 28:18-20)

Soon after He gave them their commission, He "was snatched up to God and to his throne" (Rev. 12:5). While the disciples were watching, "he was taken up before their very eyes, and a cloud hid him from their sight" (Acts 1:9).

This newly organized apostolic church grew very rapidly, baptizing 3,000 in one day. This rapid growth raised the need for more workers to be appointed for the church. So the apostles said to the church members,

> Brothers, choose seven men from among you who are known to be full of the Spirit and wisdom. We will turn this responsibility over to them and will give our attention to prayer and the ministry of the word. (Acts 6:3-4)

The appointment of the seven to take the oversight of special lines of work, proved a great blessing to the church.

These officers gave careful consideration to individual needs as well as to the general financial interests of the church, and by their prudent management and their godly example they were an important aid to their fellow officers in binding together the various interests of the church into a united whole.

That this step was in the order of God, is revealed in the immediate results for good that were seen. "The word of God increased; and the number of the disciples multiplied in Jerusalem greatly; and a great company of the priests were obedient to the faith." (*The Acts of the Apostles*, 89-90)

Satan, knowing that Jesus had gained the victory over him by His death on the cross, and seeing the rapid growth of the church, became alarmed that he was losing control over the people of this earth. In desperation, "he pursued the woman [the true church] who had given birth to the male child" (Rev. 12:13).

Very early in the development of the Christian church, Satan began his attack on the purity and character of the woman (this true church) who was standing on the moon, clothed with the sun of righteousness. Jesus Himself warned the disciples to be on the alert, for deceivers and false prophets would enter the church. He said, "Watch out that no one deceives you. For many will come in my name, claiming, 'I am the Christ,' and will deceive many." "At that time many will turn away from the faith and will betray and hate each other, and many false prophets will appear and deceive many people. Because of the increase of wickedness, the love of most will grow cold, but he who stands firm to the end will be saved." (Matt. 24:4-5, 10-13)

The extent and seriousness of the apostasy is witnessed by the fact that all the New Testament writers speak of this problem.

Paul counseled the Thessalonians saying, "Let no man deceive you by any means: for *that day shall not come*, except there come a falling away first, and that man of sin be revealed, the son of perdition." (2 Thess. 2:3, KJV) (Emphasis supplied.)

To the Galatians, he writes, "I am astonished that you are so quickly deserting the one who called you by the grace of Christ and are turning to a different gospel—which is really no gospel at all. Evidently some people are throwing you into confusion and are trying to pervert the gospel of Christ." (Gal. 1:6-7)

Paul discusses the subject in both of his letters to Timothy. In his second letter to Timothy, he warns,

> But know this, that in the last days perilous times will come: For men will be lovers of themselves, lovers of money, boasters, proud, blasphemers, disobedient to parents, unthankful, unholy, unloving, unforgiving, slanderers, without self-control, brutal, despisers of good, traitors, headstrong, haughty, lovers of pleasure rather than lovers of God, having a form of godliness but denying its power. And from such people turn away! (2 Tim. 3:1-5, NKJV)

Peter indicates that many will become involved in this apostasy.

> But there were also false prophets among the people, even as there will be false teachers among you, who will secretly bring in destructive heresies, even denying the Lord who bought them, and bring on themselves swift destruction. And many will follow their destructive ways, because of whom the way of truth will be blasphemed. By covetousness they will exploit you with deceptive words. (2 Pet. 2:1-3, NKJV)

Luke, who traveled with Paul much of the time, tells of Paul's instruction to the Ephesian church.

> For I know this, that after my departure savage wolves will come in among you, not sparing the flock. Also from among yourselves men will rise up, speaking perverse things, to draw away the disciples after themselves. Therefore watch, and remember that for three years I did not cease to warn everyone night and day with tears. (Acts 20:29-31, NKJV)

Jude very graphically describes these apostate leaders.

> Beloved, while I was very diligent to write to you concerning our common salvation, I found it necessary to write to you exhorting you to contend earnestly for the faith which was once for all delivered to the saints. For certain men have crept in unnoticed, who long ago were marked out for this

> condemnation, ungodly men, who turn the grace of our God into lewdness and deny the only Lord God and our Lord Jesus Christ. (Jude 3-4, NKJV) They are clouds without water, carried about by the winds; late autumn trees without fruit, twice dead, pulled up by the roots; raging waves of the sea, foaming up their own shame; wandering stars for whom is reserved the blackness of darkness forever. (Jude 12-13)

The apostle John refers to this great apostasy as the spirit of the Antichrist.

> Beloved, do not believe every spirit, but test the spirits, whether they are of God; because many false prophets have gone out into the world. By this you know the Spirit of God: Every spirit that confesses that Jesus Christ has come in the flesh is of God, and every spirit that does not confess that Jesus Christ has come in the flesh is not of God. And this is the *spirit* of the Antichrist, which you have heard was coming, and is now already in the world. (1 John 4:1-3, NKJV)

There are many more texts that could be cited by these writers, which give evidence of Satan's ruthless attack on that early apostolic church. His pursuit of the woman continued for centuries until only a remnant of faithful believers was left.

There is another very graphic description of Satan's war against this young Christian church. It is found in Revelation 6.

> I watched as the Lamb opened the first of the seven seals. Then I heard one of the four living creatures say in a voice like thunder, "Come!" I looked, and there before me was a white horse! Its rider held a bow, and he was given a crown, and he rode out as a conqueror bent on conquest.
>
> When the Lamb opened the second seal, I heard the second living creature say, "Come!" Then another horse came out, a fiery red one. Its rider was given power to take peace from the earth and to make men slay each other. To him was given a large sword.
>
> When the Lamb opened the third seal, I heard the third living creature say, "Come!" I looked, and there before me

was a black horse! Its rider was holding a pair of scales in his
hand. Then I heard what sounded like a voice among the four
living creatures, saying, "A quart of wheat for a day's wages,
and three quarts of barley for a day's wages, and do not damage
the oil and the wine!"

When the Lamb opened the fourth seal, I heard the voice
of the fourth living creature say, "Come!" I looked, and there
before me was a pale horse! Its rider was named Death, and
Hades was following close behind him. They were given power
over a fourth of the earth to kill by sword, famine and plague,
and by the wild beasts of the earth. (Rev. 6:1-8)

Because the first horse is white, there are some who believe that the
first seal is a depiction of the Christian church going forth to conquer
the world for Christ. There are at least three reasons why this cannot be
a correct interpretation of these verses. When the weight of evidence is
considered, it will be seen that these four seals reveal Satan's attack on
the apostolic church during which time he turned it into the "synagogue
of Satan" (Rev. 2:9; 3:9).

1. There are two things that are common to the first four seals. They
    are the riders and the horses. The item that changes in each seal
    is the color of the horse. It should be noted that the color does not
    include the rider. There is no evidence to support the view that the
    rider represents two different beings, such as Christ in the first
    seal and Satan in other seals. The rider is simply unidentified in
    the first three seals, but he is finally identified in the fourth seal.
2. The fact that the rider is unidentified is a second reason that he
    does not represent Christ. Christ never works in secret. He always
    identifies Himself. He wants everyone to know who He is so they
    can come to Him with their sins and have them washed away with
    His blood. He says, "I have spoken openly to the world; I always
    taught in synagogues, and in the temple, where all the Jews come
    together; and I spoke nothing in secret." (John 18:20, NASB)
3. A third reason that these riders do not represent Christ is that they
    are bent on conquest by force. They are all riding horses, which in
    scripture represent conquest and war. The first rider is carrying a
    bow, a weapon of war, and is bent on conquest by force. The second
    rider held a large sword and took peace from the earth and caused

men to slay each other. The third rider had a pair of scales (balances) in his hand. The fourth rider named Death, with Hades following him, was given power to kill by sword, famine, and plague.

These four riders have the same objective—to rule by force. To rule by force is foreign to the government of heaven. The government of heaven is ruled by love. God loved the world so much that He gave His Son to redeem it. By self-sacrificing love, Jesus gained the victory over Satan when He gave His life on the cross. These riders are performing just the opposite to the principles of heaven.

In the fourth seal, Death is personified to represent Satan, the originator or cause of death in this world. Hades is personified to represent all the forces of evil—that is all of the fallen angels. It could also include all the other followers of Satan.

When Satan began his attack on the young Christian church, it had a pure message of truth represented by the color of the first horse. The central message of the church was Jesus, the Lamb of God, who gave His life for the sins of the world. They told how He ascended to heaven to open the holy place of the sanctuary in heaven to begin His work as our advocate and high priest to receive and remove the confessed sins of His people on earth. Satan was so successful in obliterating this doctrine that by AD 1844 no one on the earth knew that there was a sanctuary in heaven. We will study more about this in the next chapter.

The apostolic church did not long remain in this pure state of truth. As we cited above, all the writers of the New Testament were concerned about the false prophets, the deceivers, and the errors that were creeping into the church. This phenomenon is represented by the red color of the second horse, red being a symbol of sin (Isa. 1:18).

The third horse is colored black. In the Bible, black represents a condition in which there is an absence of light—the light of truth. At the time of the third seal, the church had drifted so far into sin that God could find no light of truth left in it. And like Belshazzar of ancient Babylon, there comes a time when God will weigh our characters in the balances of the sanctuary. If the one weighed is found wanting, God casts him or her aside. That is what happened to the apostolic church.

During the time of the third seal (Rev. 6:5)—the third horse—the light of truth was turned into error, but "the archdeceiver had not completed his work. He was resolved to gather the Christian world under his banner and to exercise his power through his vicegerent, the proud pontiff who claimed to be the representative of Christ. Through half-converted pagans, ambitious prelates, and world-loving churchmen he accomplished his purpose." (*The Great Controversy*, 53)

In the time of the fourth seal (Rev. 6:7-8), we see Death (Satan) and Hades (fallen angels) in charge of the church. Professing to be Christian, this once-pure church had come under the leadership of Satan.

They were given power over a fourth of the earth to kill by sword, famine and plague, and by the wild beasts of the earth. (Rev. 6:8)

> In the sixth century the papacy had become firmly established. Its seat of power was fixed in the imperial city, and the bishop of Rome was declared to be the head over the entire church. Paganism had given place to the papacy. The dragon had given to the beast "his power, and his seat, and great authority." Revelation 13:2. And now began the 1260 years of papal oppression foretold in the prophecies of Daniel and the Revelation. Daniel 7:25; Revelation 13:5-7. Christians were forced to choose either to yield their integrity and accept the papal ceremonies and worship, or to wear away their lives in dungeons or suffer death by the rack, the fagot, or the headsman's ax. Now were fulfilled the words of Jesus: "Ye shall be betrayed both by parents, and brethren, and kinsfolks, and friends; and some of you shall they cause to be put to death. And ye shall be hated of all men for My name's sake." Luke 21:16, 17. Persecution opened upon the faithful with greater fury than ever before, and the world became a vast battlefield. For hundreds of years the church of Christ found refuge in seclusion and obscurity. Thus says the prophet: "The woman fled into the wilderness, where she hath a place prepared of God, that they should feed her there a thousand two hundred and three-score days." Revelation 12:6. (ibid., 54-55)

This power is represented as "a little horn" (Dan. 7:8, 25) who thought "to change the set times and the laws." It was during this time that the papacy changed the day of worship from the seventh-day Sabbath to Sunday—the first day of the week in fulfillment of the prophecy of Daniel 7:25. John was also shown this same power represented as a beast coming up out of the sea. See Revelation 13:1-10. The characteristics of this beast are the same as those of the little horn in Daniel 7:8, 25. The 1,260-year period in Daniel 7:25 and Revelation 12:6, 14 is the same as the forty-two months in Revelation 13:5. The papacy is also represented as a stern-faced king in Daniel 8:23. We will study more about this stern-faced king in the next chapter.

9

The Abomination of Desolation

In the previous chapter, we learned how Satan warred against the apostolic church until He completely destroyed its character and message. The faithful believers separated from its borders, and Satan had full control of the church. Satan had two major objectives in his attack on the Christian church—(1) to get the people to believe that the law was changed, or that God did away with the necessity of obeying the law after Jesus died on the cross, and (2) to lead the people to forget or lose sight of their knowledge and understanding of Jesus' work as their high priest and advocate in the sanctuary in heaven.

The Bible identifies the growing apostasy of the apostolic church as the "synagogue of Satan" (Rev. 2:9). The members of Satan's church are the children of disobedience. The work and activities of Satan's church are described as follows:

> It grew until it reached the host of the heavens, and it threw some of the starry host down to the earth and trampled on them. It set itself up to be as great as the Prince of the host; it took away the daily sacrifice* from him, and the place of his sanctuary was brought low. Because of rebellion, the host of the saints and the daily sacrifice* were given over to it. It prospered in everything it did, and truth was thrown to the ground. (Dan. 8:10-12)

After Satan had achieved his objectives as described above, a holy one asked, "How long will it take for the vision to be fulfilled—the vision concerning the daily sacrifice,* the rebellion that causes desolation,

---

* The word *sacrifice* in Daniel 8:11-13 is not in the original manuscripts.

and the surrender of the sanctuary and of the host that will be trampled underfoot?" (Dan. 8:13)

The answer was given. "He said to me, 'It will take 2,300 evenings and mornings; then the sanctuary will be reconsecrated'" (Dan. 8:14).

Other Bible translations say that the sanctuary will be "restored to its rightful state" (NRSV); "cleansed" (KJV); "vindicated" (MKJV); or "properly restored" (NASB).

Daniel did not understand the vision, so the angel Gabriel was sent to explain the vision to him.

> "Son of man," he said to me, "understand that the vision concerns the time of the end." (Dan. 8:17)
>
> He said: "I am going to tell you what will happen later in the time of wrath, because the vision concerns the appointed time of the end. The two-horned ram that you saw represents the kings of Media and Persia. The shaggy goat is the king of Greece, and the large horn between his eyes is the first king. The four horns that replaced the one that was broken off represent four kingdoms that will emerge from his nation but will not have the same power.
>
> "In the latter part of their reign, when rebels have become completely wicked, a stern-faced king, a master of intrigue, will arise. He will become very strong, but not by his own power. He will cause astounding devastation and will succeed in whatever he does. He will destroy the mighty men and the holy people. He will cause deceit to prosper, and he will consider himself superior. When they feel secure, he will destroy many and take his stand against the Prince of princes. Yet he will be destroyed, but not by human power.
>
> "The vision of the evenings and mornings that has been given you is true, but seal up the vision, for it concerns the distant future." (Dan. 8:19-26)

In the study of this vision, it is important to recognize what part of the vision Daniel did not understand and why it was of such concern to him. The portion of the vision recorded in Daniel 8:1-8 and its interpretation in verses 19-22 was not difficult for him to understand. As a high official in the nation of Babylon, Daniel had become well acquainted with the nation of Medo-Persia and its rulers. Just a few years after this vision, he himself would be a high official in that kingdom. He must have also had knowledge of the growing Grecian territory far to the west. The rise and fall of these nations was already taking place before him, so he could not have been appalled by this part of the vision nor was it beyond his understanding.

The part of the vision that was so perplexing to Daniel is recorded in Daniel 8:9-14 and its interpretation given by the angel Gabriel in verses 23 to 26. There were three things in this part of the vision that caused Daniel much concern—(1) When would all the things mentioned in these verses take place? (2) Who was represented by the horn that started small—the stern-faced king in verse 23—that caused so much destruction of the sanctuary, destroyed the holy people, and even took a stand against the Prince of princes? And (3) what did it mean that the sanctuary would be reconsecrated in 2,300 evenings and mornings?

We will study these three items in the order given above.

When will all the things in Daniel 8:9-14 take place?

There are five phrases that tell when this vision would be fulfilled.

1. Verse 17—"The vision concerns the time of the end"
2. Verse 19—"Later in the time of wrath"
3. Verse 19—"The appointed time of the end"
4. Verse 23—"In the latter part of their reign"
5. Verse 26—"It concerns the distant future"

Five times in these verses we are told that this vision refers to the "time of the end," the "distant future." Near the end of the ministry of Jesus, the disciples asked Him, "What will be the sign of your coming and the end of the age?" (Matt. 24:3) By outlining a series of events in Matthew 24, Jesus tried to help His disciples realize that the "time of the end" was still far into the future. Therefore, we can know that the fulfillment of these verses would come some time after the first advent of Christ.

Who is represented by the horn that grew slowly?

Who is this horn that grew slowly—the stern-faced king, the one that caused so much desolation? Let us look at the similarities between the information given in the vision and those given in the angel Gabriel's interpretation. In the chart below, the phrases in Daniel 8:9-12 will be listed under the heading "Vision" and the similar phrases in verses 23-25 will be listed under the heading "Interpretation."

Vision	Interpretation
V. 9— Out of one of them came another horn which started small but grew into power	V. 23—A stern-faced king, a master of intrigue, will arise.
V. 10—It grew until it reached the host of the heavens	V. 25—He will consider himself superior.
V. 10—It threw some of the starry host down to earth and trampled them	V. 24—He will destroy the mighty men and the holy people.
V. 11—It set itself up to be as great as the Prince of the host	V. 25—He will take his stand against the Prince of princes.
V. 11—It took away the daily from him and the place of his sanctuary was brought low	V. 24—He will cause astounding devastation.
V. 12—Because of rebellion the daily and the saints were given over to it	V. 23—When the rebels have become completely wicked, a stern-faced king will arise.
V. 12—It prospered in everything it did	V. 24—He will succeed in whatever he does.
V. 12—Truth was thrown to the ground	V. 25—He will cause deceit to prosper.

It is readily observed from the similar phrases in this chart that the power represented in Daniel 8:9-12 is the same as that described in verses 23-25.

Having already seen that Daniel 8:23-25 applies to the time of the Christian church, verses 9-12 would also apply to this same period and to the same power.

In the previous chapter, we noted that all of the New Testament writers warned of the apostasy and false teachers that were even then coming into the apostolic church. We will now turn to these writers and see how many of the above items are brought to light in their warnings.

The *first point* we will look for is this: "Is there evidence of the rise of a power that had the characteristics of the small horn, the stern-faced king?" A few days before Jesus was crucified, the disciples asked Him, "What will be the sign of your coming and of the end of the age?" (Matt. 24:3) He replied, "Watch out that you are not deceived. For many will come in my name, claiming, 'I am he,' and, 'The time is near.' Do not follow them." (Luke 21:8)

Jesus told the disciples plainly that the time was near when a new element would come into the young church. Like the stern-faced king, these people would deceive others and claim to be Jesus and to speak in His name. Christ warned the disciples, "Do not follow them."

The *second point* refers to this power considering itself superior. The references below are evidence that those leading the apostasy in the Christian church considered themselves superior. Paul is very specific to Timothy about the developing apostasy.

> But mark this: There will be terrible times in the last days. People will be lovers of themselves, lovers of money, *boastful, proud*, abusive, disobedient to their parents, ungrateful, unholy, without love, unforgiving, slanderous, without self-control, brutal, not lovers of the good, treacherous, rash, *conceited*, lovers of pleasure rather than lovers of God—*having a form of godliness* but denying its power. (2 Tim. 3:1-5) (Emphasis supplied.)

Like Jesus, Paul warns Timothy, "Have nothing to do with them."

In his letter to the church at Thessalonica, Paul said this "man of lawlessness" will "exalt himself over everything that is called God or is worshiped, so that he sets himself up in God's temple, proclaiming himself to be God" (2 Thess. 2:3-4).

Jude says, "These men are grumblers and faultfinders; they follow their own evil desires; they *boast about themselves* and flatter others *for their own advantage*" (Jude 16). (Emphasis supplied.)

The *third point* in the chart revealed that this power would be a persecuting power. In Daniel 8:24, we are told that this stern-faced king would "destroy the mighty men and the holy people." Notice how accurately Jesus portrays the fulfillment of this prophecy.

> Then you will be handed over to be persecuted and put to death, and you will be hated by all nations because of me. At that time many will turn away from the faith and will betray

and hate each other, and many false prophets will appear and deceive many people. (Matt. 24:9-11)

In the *fourth point*, we read that this power would "set itself up to be as great as the Prince of the host" and would "take his stand against the Prince of princes." In his second letter to the Thessalonians, Paul warns them:

> Don't let anyone deceive you in any way, for that day will not come until the rebellion occurs and the man of lawlessness is revealed, the man doomed to destruction. He will oppose and will exalt himself over everything that is called God or is worshiped, so that he sets himself up in God's temple, proclaiming himself to be God. (2 Thess. 2:3-4)

This is an exact fulfillment of the description given in Daniel 8. Later in the chapter, you will see how this stern-faced king "sets himself up in God's temple, proclaiming himself to be God."

Jude adds, "For certain men whose condemnation was written about long ago have secretly slipped in among you. They are godless men, who change the grace of our God into a license for immorality and deny Jesus Christ our only Sovereign and Lord" (Jude 4).

In the *fifth point*, we found that this power "took away the daily . . . from Him, and the place of His sanctuary was brought low," which would "cause astounding devastation" (Dan. 8:11, 24).

In chapter 7, we studied about the opening of the sanctuary in heaven when Jesus ascended. Satan realized that as long as the people knew about the ministry of Jesus in the sanctuary in heaven for the removal of their sins, he would lose many people from his control. He must obliterate this doctrine from the minds of the people. The following is a concise description of how the stern-faced king went about this work.

> The accession of the Roman Church to power marked the beginning of the Dark Ages. As her power increased, the darkness deepened. Faith was transferred from Christ, the true foundation, to the pope of Rome. Instead of trusting in the Son of God for forgiveness of sins and for eternal salvation, the people looked to the pope, and to the priests and prelates to whom he delegated authority. They were taught that the pope

was their earthly mediator and that none could approach God
except through him. (*The Great Controversy*, 55)

The devastation to Christ's ministry in the heavenly sanctuary caused
by this religio-political power cannot be fully comprehended.

The *sixth point* reiterates that this power will be a persecuting power
and that it would become "completely wicked."

In the rebellion of the stern-faced king, when the rebels had become
"completely wicked," the saints were given over to him and heavily
persecuted. Jesus warned the disciples concerning this persecution to
come into the Christian church.

> They will lay hands on you and persecute you. They will
> deliver you to synagogues and prisons, and you will be brought
> before kings and governors, and all on account of my name.
> You will be betrayed even by parents, brothers, relatives and
> friends, and they will put some of you to death. All men will
> hate you because of me. (Luke 21:12, 16-17)

Paul, in his farewell comments to the Ephesian church, warned them
of the rebellion that would come into their church.

> I know that after I leave, savage wolves will come in among
> you and will not spare the flock. Even from your own number
> men will arise and distort the truth in order to draw away
> disciples after them. (Acts 20:29-30)

In the *seventh point*, we found that the stern-faced king will prosper
and succeed in whatever he does. Peter says,

> But there were also false prophets among the people, just
> as there will be false teachers among you. They will secretly
> introduce destructive heresies, even denying the sovereign Lord
> who bought them—bringing swift destruction on themselves.
> Many will follow their shameful ways and will bring the way
> of truth into disrepute. (2 Pet. 2:1-2)

Paul, when writing to the Thessalonian church concerning "the man
of lawlessness," warned, "He will oppose and will exalt himself over

everything that is called God or is worshiped, so that he sets himself up in God's temple, proclaiming himself to be God" (2 Thess. 2:3-4).

> Little by little, at first in stealth and silence, and then more openly as it increased in strength and gained control of the minds of men, "the mystery of iniquity" carried forward its deceptive and blasphemous work . . . . The nominal conversion of Constantine, in the early part of the fourth century, caused great rejoicing; and the world, cloaked with a form of righteousness, walked into the church.
>
> This compromise between paganism and Christianity resulted in the development of "the man of sin" foretold in prophecy as opposing and exalting himself above God. That gigantic system of false religion is a masterpiece of Satan's power—a monument of his efforts to seat himself upon the throne to rule the earth according to his will. (ibid., 49-50)
>
> The great apostate had succeeded in exalting himself "above all that is called God, or that is worshiped." 2 Thessalonians 2:4. (ibid., 53)
>
> In the sixth century the papacy had become firmly established. Its seat of power was fixed in the imperial city, and the bishop of Rome was declared to be the head over the entire church. Paganism had given place to the papacy. The dragon had given to the beast "his power, and his seat, and great authority." Revelation 13:2. And now began the 1260 years of papal oppression foretold in the prophecies of Daniel and the Revelation. Daniel 7:25; Revelation 13:5-7. (ibid., 54)
>
> The accession of the Roman Church to power marked the beginning of the Dark Ages. As her power increased, the darkness deepened. (ibid., 55)

The *eighth point* revealed that during his rebellion the stern-faced king would throw truth to the ground and cause deceit to prosper. Paul opens his letter to the Galatians by saying,

> I am astonished that you are so quickly deserting the one who called you by the grace of Christ and are turning to a different gospel—which is really no gospel at all. Evidently

some people are throwing you into confusion and are trying to pervert the gospel of Christ. (Gal. 1:6-7)

The apostle Peter also prophesied that truth would be cast aside and warned the people about this apostasy.

> There were also false prophets among the people, just as there will be false teachers among you. They will secretly introduce destructive heresies, even denying the sovereign Lord who bought them—bringing swift destruction on themselves. Many will follow their shameful ways and will bring the way of truth into disrepute. In their greed these teachers will exploit you with stories they have made up. (2 Pet. 2:1-3)
>
> Among the leading causes that had led to the separation of the true church from Rome was the hatred of the latter toward the Bible Sabbath. As foretold by prophecy, the papal power cast down the truth to the ground. The law of God was trampled in the dust, while the traditions and customs of men were exalted. (ibid., 65)

All eight characteristics and activities of the "horn which started small" and the "stern-faced king" have been clearly documented as being a part of the apostasy of the apostolic church. Over time, the rebellion grew so large that this apostate church assumed official control of the whole Christian world in AD 538 and took on the name *Roman Catholic Church*. In Revelation 12:6, 14, John says that this church would remain in power for the next 1,260 years.

We mentioned at the beginning of this chapter that Satan had two objectives—to negate the law of God and to wipe out the knowledge that Jesus was making an atonement for every true believer and working as their advocate at the throne of God in the heavenly sanctuary. The weight of evidence from history concerning these two items overwhelmingly points to the horn that grew slowly and the stern-faced king as symbols depicting the apostasy of the apostolic church that developed into the Roman Catholic Church.

What does it mean that the sanctuary will be "reconsecrated" in 2,300 days?

There is a third item that we need to study in Daniel 8.

> Then I heard a holy one speaking, and another holy one said to him, "How long will it take for the vision to be fulfilled—the vision concerning the daily . . . , the rebellion that causes desolation and the surrender of the sanctuary and of the host that will be trampled underfoot?" He said to me, "It will take 2,300 evenings and mornings; then the sanctuary will be reconsecrated." (Dan. 8:13-14)

There are three questions that we need to ask as we look at these verses: (1) What is "the rebellion that causes desolation, and the surrender of the sanctuary," (2) What are the beginning and ending dates for this time prophecy, and (3) What does it mean when it says the sanctuary will be "reconsecrated"? As we close this chapter, we will look at just the first question—what is the "rebellion that causes desolation"? We will consider the other two questions in future chapters.

The "rebellion that causes desolation" of this sanctuary is also called the "abomination of desolation" in some Bible translations. The "reconsecration" of this sanctuary is referred to in other translations as the restoration of the sanctuary "to its rightful state."

We know from the context of this passage of scripture that the rebellion is developed before the reconsecration of the sanctuary. We also found that this rebellion that causes desolation of the sanctuary follows the first advent of Jesus and that it is associated with the apostasy of the Christian church that was raised up by the apostles.

In the study of "The Two Sanctuaries," chapter 6, we learned that one sanctuary was located on the earth, and that this sanctuary was a pattern of the one in heaven. The sanctuary that is the subject of Daniel 8 could not be the one on earth. Just before Jesus was crucified, He told the Jews, "Your house is left to you desolate" (Matt. 23:38).

> Hitherto He had called the temple His Father's house; but now, as the Son of God should pass out from those walls, God's presence would be withdrawn forever from the temple built to His glory. Henceforth its ceremonies would be meaningless, its services a mockery. (*The Desire of Ages*, 620)

This sanctuary was completely destroyed by the Romans in AD 70. The question is, how could the stern-faced king that has been identified in the previous chapter as the Roman Catholic Church, or the papacy, cause such devastation of the sanctuary in heaven?

In chapter 7 we learned that when Jesus ascended to heaven, He immediately opened the holy place of the sanctuary. Revelation 4 and 5 give us a description of the celebration that took place at this time. Paul says, "For Christ did not enter a man-made sanctuary that was only a copy of the true one; he entered heaven itself, now to appear for us in God's presence" (Heb. 9:24). This was electrifying news to that early apostolic church. The Jews had been offering lambs for more than 1,400 years, believing that in those sacrifices was the promise of a Redeemer. The lambs had no power to save them or to relieve them of the guilt of their sins.

But now the Lamb of God had come. The disciples had seen Him offer Himself on the cross. They had watched His blood flow for the remission of their sins. They had seen and talked with Him after He rose from the grave, and they had watched as He ascended to heaven.

> They knew that they had a Representative in heaven, an Advocate at the throne of God. In solemn awe they bowed in prayer, repeating the assurance, "Whatsoever ye shall ask the Father in My name, He will give it you." . . . John 16:23. Higher and still higher they extended the hand of faith, with the mighty argument, "It is Christ that died, yea rather, that is risen again, who is even at the right hand of God, who also maketh intercession for us." Romans 8:34. (*The Acts of the Apostles*, 35-36)

This was the central pillar of the message that the apostles took to the world, and because the Jews had rejected Jesus as the Lamb of God and did not know that He had ascended to the heavenly sanctuary to intercede for repentant sinners, they complained that the apostles had "turned the world upside down" (Acts 17:6, RSV). Now the question comes to mind, Why was it that when the first angel's message was proclaimed at the beginning of the great second advent movement, no one on earth knew where the sanctuary was located? Why did every one think that the earth was the sanctuary?

The reason becomes very clear in the following quotations:

> In the sixth century the papacy had become firmly established. Its seat of power was fixed in the imperial city, and the bishop of Rome was declared to be the head over the entire church. (*The Great Controversy*, 54)
>
> The accession of the Roman Church to power marked the beginning of the Dark Ages. As her power increased, the darkness deepened. *Faith was transferred from Christ, the true foundation, to the pope of Rome. Instead of trusting in the Son of God for forgiveness of sins and for eternal salvation, the people looked to the pope, and to the priests and prelates to whom he delegated authority. They were taught that the pope was their earthly mediator and that none could approach God except through him; and, further, that he stood in the place of God to them and was therefore to be implicitly obeyed.* A deviation from his requirements was sufficient cause for the severest punishment to be visited upon the bodies and souls of the offenders. *Thus the minds of the people were turned away from God to fallible, erring, and cruel men,* nay, more, to the prince of darkness himself, who exercised his power through them. Sin was disguised in a garb of sanctity. When the Scriptures are suppressed, and man comes to regard himself as supreme, we need look only for fraud, deception, and debasing iniquity . . . .
>
> *They were taught not only to look to the pope as their mediator, but to trust to works of their own to atone for sin.* (ibid., 55) (Emphasis supplied.)

In this work of the papacy during the long period of the 1,260 years is seen the fulfillment of Daniel's prophecy of the abomination or rebellion that causes desolation (Dan. 8:13). God the Father, the Creator of the universe, had sacrificed His only begotten Son. Christ, who had stood by the side of His Father throughout eternity, had voluntarily offered His own life to redeem the fallen race. How could such ingratitude be described more accurately than to call it the "abomination that causes desolation"?

10

Dating the 2,300 Evenings and Mornings

Near the close of the last chapter, three questions were raised regarding "the rebellion that causes desolation." We answered the first question—what is this rebellion or abomination? The second question is, when would this rebellion take place? We will answer that question in this chapter by briefly reviewing three time prophecies found in Daniel 7, 8, and 9.

There are two important principles to consider when studying time prophecies.

1. A day symbolizes a year (Num. 14:34; Ezek. 4:6).
2. A month is considered to be thirty days (Gen. 7:11, 24, 8:3-4).

The prophecy concerning the "2,300 evenings and mornings" (Dan. 8:14) is the most important time prophecy in the Bible. Very closely connected to it is the seventy-week time prophecy found in Daniel 9:24. We want to know how these two prophecies are connected to each other and how they relate to the sanctuary on the earth and to the sanctuary in heaven.

In 551 BC, the angel Gabriel related to Daniel the vision concerning the desolation of the sanctuary recorded in Daniel 8. Gabriel said that it would be 2,300 evenings and mornings (days) before it would be restored to its rightful place. When closing the vision, he told Daniel, "The vision of the evenings and mornings that has been given you is true, but seal up the vision, for it concerns the distant future." When Daniel awoke from his vision, he commented that he "was appalled by the vision" and that "it was beyond his understanding" (Dan. 8:26-27).

In 539 BC, about twelve years later, Gabriel returned to give Daniel more understanding of the vision concerning the sanctuary. He said to

Daniel, "I have now come to give you insight and understanding . . . . Therefore, consider the message and understand the vision" (Dan. 9:22-23).

Gabriel begins his explanation with this statement, "Seventy 'sevens' [weeks] are decreed [cut off] for your people and your holy city to finish transgression" (Dan. 9:24).

From what were the seventy weeks cut off? It would have to be from the longer time prophecy, the 2,300 days mentioned in Daniel 8:14 as there is no other time prophecy given in this context from which to cut it off, and Gabriel was specifically sent to Daniel to explain the vision he had seen as recorded in Daniel 8.

Gabriel next informed Daniel that the seventy weeks would be dated "from the issuing of the decree to restore and rebuild Jerusalem" (Dan. 9:25). This decree is recorded in Ezra 7:12-26. It was implemented in the autumn of 457 BC.

> Taking this as the starting point, there was perfect harmony in the application of all the events foretold in the explanation of that period in Daniel 9:25-27. Sixty-nine weeks, the first 483 of the 2,300 years, were to reach to the Messiah, the Anointed One; and Christ's baptism and anointing by the Holy Spirit, A.D. 27, exactly fulfilled the specification. In the midst of the seventieth week, Messiah was to be cut off. Three and a half years after His baptism, Christ was crucified, in the spring of A.D. 31. The seventy weeks, or 490 years, were to pertain especially to the Jews. At the expiration of this period the nation sealed its rejection of Christ by the persecution of His disciples, and the apostles turned to the Gentiles, A.D. 34. The first 490 years of the 2,300 having then ended, 1810 years would remain. From A.D. 34, 1810 years extend to 1844. "Then," said the angel, "shall the sanctuary be cleansed." (*The Great Controversy*, 410)

Below are diagrams of the two time prophecies with dates and explanations.

Seventy "Sevens" (Weeks) Diagram
Daniel 9:24
70 x 7 = 490 days (years)

70 weeks-490 years		
7 weeks	3 score and 2 (62) weeks	1 week 7 years
49 years	434 years	3 ½ years | 3 ½ years

457 BC	408 BC		AD 27	AD 31	AD 34
(1)	(2)		(3)	(4)	(5)

History confirms the interpretation and dates of this time prophecy. Using the day for a year principle, the 490-day prophecy, being a part of the 2,300-day prophecy of Daniel 8:14, establishes 457 BC as the beginning date for the 2,300-day prophecy. The ending date is then AD 1844.

(1) Command to restore and rebuild Jerusalem (Ezra 7:12-26)
(2) City and temple rebuilt (may refer to Neh. 12:27-43)
(3) Baptism and anointing of Jesus (Matt. 3:13-17; Mark 1:9-11; Luke 3:21-22; John 1:29-34)
(4) Jesus crucified (Matt. 27:32-54; Mark 15:21-39; Luke 23:26-47; John 19:17-37)
(5) Stephen stoned (Acts 7:54-60); Gospel goes to the Gentiles (Acts 8:4-40)

2,300-Day (Year) Prophecy Diagram
Daniel 8:14

2,300 days (years)	
490 days (years)	1810 days (years)

457 BC	AD 34	AD 1844

The meaning of the 2,300-day (year) period was not given to Daniel. His book was shut up and sealed until the time of the end (Dan. 12:9). In subsequent chapters, we will consider the importance of this time prophecy and its significance for us today.

Before closing this chapter, we will study the relationship of the 1,260-year time prophecy as mentioned in Daniel 7:25 to the two time prophecies already presented.

> He will speak against the Most High and oppress his saints and try to change the set times and the laws. The saints will be handed over to him for a time, times and half a time. (Dan. 7:25)

There are three phrases in Bible prophecy that refer to this same period.

1. 1,260 days (years) (Rev. 12:6, 11:3)
2. 42 months (30 days/month) (Rev. 13:5; 11:2)
3. Time, times, and half a time (Dan. 7:25, 12:7; Rev. 12:14)

    a. A time represents a year (360 days in the Hebrew calendar)
    b. Times represent two years
    c. Half a time represents half a year

Daniel 12:7 and Revelation 12:6, 14, are in reference to the dragon pursuing the woman (true church) into the desert, and Revelation 13:5 is in connection with the beast coming out of the sea.

We found in chapters 8 and 9 that the beginning of this 1,260-year period was AD 538. But what event marked its close?

> "Power was given unto him to continue forty and two months." And, says the prophet, "I saw one of his heads as it were wounded to death." And again: "He that leadeth into captivity shall go into captivity: he that killeth with the sword must be killed with the sword." The forty and two months are the same as the "time and times and the dividing of time," three years and a half, or 1,260 days, of Daniel 7—the time during which the papal power was to oppress God's people. This period, as stated in preceding chapters, began with the supremacy of the papacy, A.D. 538, and terminated in 1798. At that time the pope was made captive by the French army,

the papal power received its deadly wound, and the prediction was fulfilled, "He that leadeth into captivity shall go into captivity." (ibid., 439)

The weight of evidence shows that the "little-horn" power in Daniel 7, the beast out of the sea in Revelation 13 and the dragon pursuing the woman into the desert in Revelation 12 are all connected with the "abomination of desolation" described in Daniel 8.

It was during this 1,260-year period—AD 538 to AD 1798—that the "abomination of desolation" took place. Thus the abomination of desolation was primarily applicable to the latter part of the 2,300-year period as shown in the diagram below.

Relationship between the 2,300-Day (Year) Prophecy
and the 1,260-Day (Year) Prophecy
Daniel 8:14; 7:25

2300 days (years)		
70 weeks or 490 days (years)	1260 days (years)	
	1810 years	

457 BC   AD 34   538   1798   1844

There is another important factor to consider in relationship to this little horn that would rule the world for 1,260 years. God's Word tells us that this power would receive a "deadly wound," but that this "deadly wound" would be healed (Rev. 13:3, 12, KJV).

This is important information to keep in mind. We will see later in this book that the "abomination of desolation" will be repeated in the near future.

We have now answered the second question raised near the end of chapter 9—when would this abomination of desolation, this attack against the heavenly sanctuary where Christ is ministering in our behalf, take place? In the next chapter, we will answer the third question—what does it mean when it says that the sanctuary will be cleansed or reconsecrated or restored to its rightful place?

11

The Lamb Opens the Most Holy Place

The types which relate to the second advent must be fulfilled at the time pointed out in the symbolic service. Under the Mosaic system the cleansing of the sanctuary, or the great Day of Atonement, occurred on the tenth day of the seventh Jewish month (Leviticus 16:29-34) . . . . The tenth day of the seventh month, the great Day of Atonement, the time of the cleansing of the sanctuary, which in the year 1844 fell upon the twenty-second of October, was regarded as the time of the Lord's coming. This was in harmony with the proofs already presented that the 2300 days would terminate in the autumn. *The Great Controversy,* 399, 400.

The scripture which above all others had been both the foundation and the central pillar of the advent faith was the declaration: "Unto two thousand and three hundred days; then shall the sanctuary be cleansed." Daniel 8:14. These had been familiar words to all believers in the Lord's soon coming. By the lips of thousands was this prophecy repeated as the watchword of their faith. All felt that upon the events therein foretold depended their brightest expectations and most cherished hopes. (ibid., 409)

But the time passed, and Jesus did not come to this earth as anticipated. There was great disappointment among the believers. But "those who followed in the light of the prophetic word saw that, instead of coming to the earth at the termination of the 2300 days in 1844, Christ then entered the most holy place of the heavenly sanctuary to perform the closing work of atonement preparatory to His coming" (ibid., 422).

Daniel 8:14 (RSV) describes this event as follows:

> For two thousand and three hundred evenings and mornings;
> then the sanctuary shall be restored to its rightful state.

The subject of Christ's atoning ministry in the heavenly sanctuary, which was the central pillar of the message of the apostolic church, was abolished by the papacy during the 1,260 years. The subject of the sanctuary in heaven and Christ's atoning ministry will again be restored to its rightful place in the closing work of the great second advent movement.

There are several more passages of scripture that shed light on the subject of the sanctuary at the time of October 22, 1844. The first one we will consider is often referred to as the first angel's message.

> And he cried with a loud voice: "Fear God and give him glory, Because the hour of his judgment is come." (Rev. 14:7, MNT)
> In the typical [sacrificial] system, which was a shadow of the sacrifice and priesthood of Christ, the cleansing of the sanctuary was the last service performed by the high priest in the yearly round of ministration. It was the closing work of the atonement—a removal or putting away of sin from Israel. It prefigured the closing work in the ministration of our High Priest in heaven, in the removal or blotting out of the sins of His people, which are registered in the heavenly records. This service involves a work of investigation, a work of judgment; and it immediately precedes the coming of Christ in the clouds of heaven with power and great glory; for when He comes, every case has been decided. Says Jesus: "My reward is with Me, to give every man according as his work shall be." Revelation 22:12. It is this work of judgment, immediately preceding the second advent, that is announced in the first angel's message of Revelation 14:7: "Fear God, and give glory to Him; for the hour of His judgment is come." (ibid., 352)

The early advent believers now saw that there was also to be a judgment connected with the cleansing or restoration work. Daniel was shown in vision the opening of the court to begin this judgment.

> As I looked, "thrones were set in place, and the Ancient of Days took his seat. His clothing was as white as snow; the hair of his head was white like wool. His throne was flaming with fire, and its wheels were all ablaze. A river of fire was flowing, coming out from before him. Thousands upon thousands attended him; ten thousand times ten thousand stood before him. The court was seated, and the books were opened." (Dan. 7:9-10)

The Ancient of Days—God the Father, the One who "so loved the world that he gave his only Son" (John 3:16, RSV)—is the presiding judge of the court.

All the heavenly hosts are witnesses. Jesus Christ is the advocate or mediator. Says Daniel, "I saw in the night visions, and behold, with the clouds of heaven there came one like a son of man, and he came to the Ancient of Days and was presented before him." (Dan. 7:13, RSV)

The disciple John provides another view in the book of Revelation concerning the opening of the judgment.

> Then I saw another mighty angel coming down from heaven. He was robed in a cloud, with a rainbow above his head; his face was like the sun, and his legs were like fiery pillars. He was holding a little scroll, which lay open in his hand. He planted his right foot on the sea and his left foot on the land, and he gave a loud shout like the roar of a lion. Then the angel I had seen standing on the sea and on the land raised his right hand to heaven. And he swore by him who lives for ever and ever, who created the heavens and all that is in them, the earth and all that is in it, and the sea and all that is in it, and said, "There will be no more delay! But in the days when the seventh angel is about to sound his trumpet, the mystery of God will be accomplished, just as he announced to his servants the prophets." (Rev. 10:1-3, 5-7)

This mighty angel is none other than Jesus Christ for only He can make an oath with the Creator. There are two points in their oath—(1) "There will be no more delay!" (2) "When the seventh angel is about to sound his trumpet, the mystery of God will be accomplished."

The Creator and His Son, Jesus Christ, have taken an oath that "There will be no more delay!" This statement means that there will be no more prophecies based on time—that is, having a date at which time they will be fulfilled, such as the 2,300 evenings and mornings, the 70 weeks, and the 1,260 years. The last prophecy based on time would be the 2,300 years, which ended on October 22, 1844.

The second thing they covenanted to do was to bring the great plan for the redemption of fallen man to completion following the sounding of the seventh trumpet. When did the seventh trumpet begin to sound?

> The seventh angel sounded his trumpet, and there were loud voices in heaven, which said: "The kingdom of the world has become the kingdom of our Lord and of his Christ, and he will reign for ever and ever." And the twenty-four elders, who were seated on their thrones before God, fell on their faces and worshiped God, saying: "We give thanks to you, Lord God Almighty, the One who is and who was, because you have taken your great power and have begun to reign. The nations were angry; and your wrath has come. The time has come for judging the dead, and for rewarding your servants the prophets and your saints and those who reverence your name, both small and great—and for destroying those who destroy the earth." Then God's temple in heaven was opened, and within his temple was seen the ark of his covenant. And there came flashes of lightning, rumblings, peals of thunder, an earthquake and a great hailstorm. (Rev. 11:15-19)

The answer to our question is found in verse 18. It says, "The time has come for judging the dead." This refers to the opening of the judgment described in Daniel 7:9, 10, and 13 when the Ancient of Days took His seat to open the court. This work of judgment began on October 22, 1844.

Verse 18 continues to give more details concerning this judgment. It says that the dead will be judged. It also says that it will be a time for rewarding the prophets and the saints and "for destroying those who destroy the earth."

Another interesting point is brought to light in verse 19. It says, "Then God's temple in heaven was opened." As noted above, these verses are talking about the judgment that began on October 22, 1844, so this phrase would also apply to that date. But what does it mean when it says that the sanctuary, or temple, in heaven was opened? We know that the sanctuary was opened when Jesus ascended to heaven in AD 31.

The next phrase, "within his temple was seen the ark of his covenant," gives a clue to this question. We know from the copy of the heavenly sanctuary, which was on this earth during Old Testament times, that the ark of the testament was located in the most holy place. Therefore, in the original sanctuary in heaven, the ark of the covenant would also be in the most holy place. So it was the door to the most holy place in the heavenly sanctuary that was opened on October 22, 1844. This would be consistent with our understanding that Jesus opened the holy place when He ascended to heaven in AD 31. Jesus ministered in the holy place until October 22, 1844, at which time He moved to the most holy place to complete His work in the heavenly sanctuary.

One other point should be noted here before we go to our next text. It was in the ark of the testimony in the most holy place of the sanctuary on earth that the law of God, written by His own finger, was kept. In the ark of the covenant in heaven, the great original is safely stored. It is now brought forth to be used as the standard in this judgment.

We have observed that on October 22, 1844, the Ancient of Days and Christ moved from the holy place to the most holy place. Jesus speaks very plainly in His message to the Philadelphia Church concerning the events taking place in the sanctuary on October 22, 1844.

> To the angel of the church in Philadelphia write: These are the words of him who is holy and true . . . . What he opens no one can shut, and what he shuts no one can open . . . . See, I have placed before you an open door that no one can shut. (Rev. 3:7-8)

We can gain some insights as to the events taking place in the heavenly sanctuary on this date by reviewing what took place in the sanctuary on earth on the Day of Atonement.

> In the service of the earthly sanctuary, which, as we have seen, is a figure of the service in the heavenly, when the high priest on the Day of Atonement entered the most holy place, the ministration in the first apartment ceased . . . . So when Christ entered the holy of holies to perform the closing work

of the atonement, He ceased His ministration in the first apartment. But when the ministration in the first apartment ended, the ministration in the second apartment began. When in the typical service the high priest left the holy on the Day of Atonement, he went in before God to present the blood of the sin offering in behalf of all Israel who truly repented of their sins. So Christ had only completed one part of His work as our intercessor, to enter upon another portion of the work, and He still pleaded His blood before the Father in behalf of sinners. (ibid., 428-429)

While it was true that that door of hope and mercy by which men had for eighteen hundred years found access to God, was closed, another door was opened, and forgiveness of sins was offered to men through the intercession of Christ in the most holy. One part of His ministration had closed, only to give place to another. There was still an "open door" to the heavenly sanctuary, where Christ was ministering in the sinner's behalf. (ibid., 429-430)

Christ had opened the door, or ministration, of the most holy place, light was shining from that open door of the sanctuary in heaven, and the fourth commandment was shown to be included in the law which is there enshrined; what God had established, no man could overthrow. (ibid., 435)

The work of Jesus in the most holy place following October 22, 1844, is clearly explained by Malachi.

"Suddenly the Lord you are seeking will come to his temple; the messenger of the covenant, whom you desire, will come," says the LORD Almighty. But who can endure the day of his coming? Who can stand when he appears? For he will be like a refiner's fire or a launderer's soap. He will sit as a refiner and purifier of silver; he will purify the Levites and refine them like gold and silver. Then the LORD will have men who will bring offerings in righteousness. (Mal. 3:1-3)

Those who are living upon the earth when the intercession of Christ shall cease in the sanctuary above are to stand in the sight of a holy God without a mediator. Their robes must be spotless, their characters must be purified from sin by the blood of sprinkling. Through the grace of God and their own diligent effort they must be conquerors in the battle with evil. While the investigative judgment is going forward in heaven, while the sins of penitent believers are being removed from the sanctuary, there is to be a special work of purification, of putting away of sin, among God's people upon earth. (ibid., 425)

In Matthew 25, we find another scripture that sheds light on the events of October 22, 1844—the parable of the ten virgins. Our attention will be on verse 6.

At midnight the cry rang out: "Here's the bridegroom! Come out to meet him!" Matthew 25:6.

In the summer and autumn of 1844 the proclamation, "Behold, the Bridegroom cometh," was given . . . .

The proclamation, "Behold, the Bridegroom cometh," in the summer of 1844, led thousands to expect the immediate advent of the Lord. At the appointed time the Bridegroom came, not to the earth, as the people expected, but to the Ancient of Days in heaven, to the marriage, the reception of His kingdom . . . .

In the parable it was those that had oil in their vessels with their lamps that went in to the marriage. Those who, with a knowledge of the truth from the Scriptures, had also the Spirit and grace of God, and who, in the night of their bitter trial, had patiently waited, searching the Bible for clearer light—these saw the truth concerning the sanctuary in heaven and the Saviour's change in ministration, and by faith they followed Him in His work in the sanctuary above. (ibid., 426-427)

In these scriptures, we have seen that the bridegroom came to the most holy place of the sanctuary in heaven on October 22, 1844. At that time, Christ opened the door to the most holy place and began the work of purifying a people to take to the wedding banquet.

In the parable of Matthew 22 the same figure of the marriage is introduced, and the investigative judgment is clearly represented as taking place before the marriage. Previous to the wedding the king comes in to see the guests, to see if all are attired in the wedding garment, the spotless robe of character washed and made white in the blood of the Lamb. Matthew 22:11; Revelation 7:14. He who is found wanting is cast out, but all who upon examination are seen to have the wedding garment on are accepted of God and accounted worthy of a share in His kingdom and a seat upon His throne. This work of examination of character, of determining who are prepared for the kingdom of God, is that of the investigative judgment, the closing work in the sanctuary above. (ibid, 428)

The light concerning the sanctuary in heaven revealed by the Lord in this chapter has much to do with the fulfillment of the prophecy, "And he said to him, 'For two thousand and three hundred evenings and mornings; then the sanctuary shall be restored to its rightful state.'" (Dan. 8:14, RSV)

The subject of the sanctuary was the key which unlocked the mystery of the disappointment of 1844. It opened to view a complete system of truth, connected and harmonious, showing that God's hand had directed the great advent movement . . . . Now in the holy of holies they again beheld Him, their compassionate High Priest, soon to appear as their king and deliverer. Light from the sanctuary illumined the past, the present, and the future. They knew that God had led them by His unerring providence. (ibid., 423)

Beginning with this chapter, a closing events time line will be included at the end of applicable chapters with the events presented in the chapter identified in their order on the time line.

Closing Events Time Line

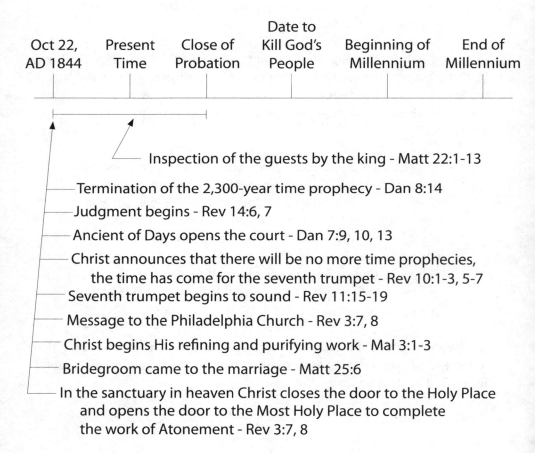

| Oct 22, AD 1844 | Present Time | Close of Probation | Date to Kill God's People | Beginning of Millennium | End of Millennium |

Inspection of the guests by the king - Matt 22:1-13

Termination of the 2,300-year time prophecy - Dan 8:14

Judgment begins - Rev 14:6, 7

Ancient of Days opens the court - Dan 7:9, 10, 13

Christ announces that there will be no more time prophecies, the time has come for the seventh trumpet - Rev 10:1-3, 5-7

Seventh trumpet begins to sound - Rev 11:15-19

Message to the Philadelphia Church - Rev 3:7, 8

Christ begins His refining and purifying work - Mal 3:1-3

Bridegroom came to the marriage - Matt 25:6

In the sanctuary in heaven Christ closes the door to the Holy Place and opens the door to the Most Holy Place to complete the work of Atonement - Rev 3:7, 8

12

The Abomination of Desolation Repeated

As we closed chapter 9, we learned that the "abomination that causes desolation" was a direct attack on the sanctuary in heaven, and that this "abomination" or "rebellion" occurred during the reign of papal supremacy during the Dark Ages, AD 538 to AD 1798. This rebellion taught the people to look to the pope, priests, and prelates for their eternal salvation instead of looking to Jesus, their high priest and mediator in the heavenly sanctuary. This rebellion was so successful that by the early nineteenth century, when the message of Daniel 8:14 was proclaimed, everyone thought that the sanctuary to be cleansed or "reconsecrated" was this earth.

Shortly after 1844, as the early advent believers continued to diligently study the scriptures, they learned that the sanctuary to be cleansed was in heaven. Through the eye of faith, they saw Jesus still mediating for the people and working to purify their characters. The message of Christ's ministry for them in the sanctuary in heaven became "the foundation and the central pillar" (*The Great Controversy*, 409) of the early advent believers. "Light from the sanctuary illumined the past, the present, and the future" (ibid., 423). It is through belief in, and the proclamation of, this message that the sanctuary is being restored to its rightful state.

For a time this message was heralded as good news. But again Satan is making an attack on this central pillar of the third angel's message in the second advent movement. How many people today are looking to Jesus in the most holy place of the sanctuary in heaven where He is performing the closing work of His ministry? The teaching that the atonement was completed at the cross and that the law of God is no longer binding has again nearly wiped out the knowledge of Christ's ministry for them in the heavenly sanctuary. But it is there, in the most holy place, that the record of every individual's life is being reviewed and compared with the law of God, that great standard of righteousness. It is there that Christ is forgiving the sins of His repentant people. It is there that He is retaining in the book of life or blotting out the name of every individual, depending on their obedience or disobedience to His law. It is there that the eternal destiny of every human being is being forever fixed.

But unlike the first abomination of desolation during the Dark Ages when the people lost the knowledge of the sanctuary in heaven, at the close of the second advent movement the knowledge of Christ's ministry in heaven will be the foundation and central pillar of the final message of mercy and warning to the world. Said the angel to the prophet Daniel, "The sanctuary will be restored to its rightful state."

In this chapter, we will study how the churches are continuing to work against the sanctuary message in the closing work of the second advent movement.

> "The temple of God was opened in heaven, and there was seen in His temple the ark of His testament." Revelation 11:19. The ark of God's testament is in the holy of holies, the second apartment of the sanctuary . . . . The announcement that the temple of God was opened in heaven and the ark of His testament was seen points to the opening of the most holy place of the heavenly sanctuary in 1844 as Christ entered there to perform the closing work of the atonement. Those who by faith followed their great High Priest as He entered upon His ministry in the most holy place beheld the ark of His testament . . . . They saw that He was now officiating before the ark of God, pleading His blood in behalf of sinners. (ibid., 433)

> The subject of the sanctuary and the investigative judgment should be clearly understood by the people of God. All need a knowledge for themselves of the position and work of their great High Priest. Otherwise it will be impossible for them to exercise the faith which is essential at this time or to occupy the position which God designs them to fill. Every individual has a soul to save or to lose. Each has a case pending at the bar of God. Each must meet the great Judge face to face. How important, then, that every mind contemplate often the solemn scene when the judgment shall sit and the books shall be opened, when, with Daniel, every individual must stand in his lot, at the end of the days. (ibid, 488)

The sanctuary in heaven is the very center of Christ's work in behalf of men. It concerns every soul living upon the earth. It opens to view the plan of redemption, bringing us down to the very close of time and revealing the triumphant issue of the contest between righteousness and sin. It is of the utmost importance that all should thoroughly investigate these subjects and be able to give an answer to everyone that asks them a reason of the hope that is in them.

The intercession of Christ in man's behalf in the sanctuary above is as essential to the plan of salvation as was His death upon the cross. By His death He began that work which after His resurrection He ascended to complete in heaven. (ibid., 488-489)

Within the holy of holies, in the sanctuary in heaven, the divine law is sacredly enshrined—the law that was spoken by God Himself amid the thunders of Sinai and written with His own finger on the tables of stone. (ibid., 434)

Those who arrived at an understanding of this important point were thus led to see the sacred, unchanging character of the divine law. They saw, as never before, the force of the Saviour's words: "Till heaven and earth pass, one jot or one tittle shall in no wise pass from the law." Matthew 5:18. *The law of God, being a revelation of His will, a transcript of His character,* must forever endure, "as a faithful witness in heaven." Not one command has been annulled; not a jot or tittle has been changed. Says the psalmist: "Forever, O Lord, Thy word is settled in heaven." "All His commandments are sure. They stand fast for ever and ever." Psalms 119:89; 111:7, 8. (ibid., 434) (Emphasis supplied.)

None could fail to see that if the earthly sanctuary was a figure or pattern of the heavenly, the law deposited in the ark on earth was an exact transcript of the law in the ark in heaven; and that an acceptance of the truth concerning the heavenly sanctuary involved an acknowledgment of the claims of God's law and the obligation of the Sabbath of the fourth commandment. Here was the secret of the bitter and determined opposition to the harmonious exposition of the Scriptures that revealed the ministration of Christ in the heavenly sanctuary. Men sought to close the door which God had opened, and to open the door which He had closed. But "He that openeth, and no man shutteth; and shutteth, and no man openeth," had declared: "Behold, I have set before thee an open door, and no man can shut it." Revelation 3:7, 8. (ibid., 435)

[In the 1830s and 1840s] the first angel's message of Revelation 14, announcing the hour of God's judgment and calling upon men to fear and worship Him, was designed to separate the professed people of God from the corrupting influences of the world and to arouse them to see their true condition of worldliness and backsliding. In this message, God has sent to the church a warning, which, had it been accepted, would have corrected the evils that were shutting them away from Him . . . .

But the churches generally did not accept the warning . . . . Multitudes, trusting implicitly to their pastors, refused to listen to the warning; and others, though convinced of the truth, dared not confess it, lest they should be "put out of the synagogue." The message which God had sent for the testing and purification of the church revealed all too surely how great was the number who had set their affections on this world rather than upon Christ. The ties which bound them to earth were stronger than the attractions heavenward. They chose to listen to the voice of worldly wisdom and turned away from the heart-searching message of truth.

In refusing the warning of the first angel, they rejected the means which Heaven had provided for their restoration. They spurned the gracious messenger that would have corrected the evils which separated them from God, and with greater eagerness they turned to seek the friendship of the world. Here was the cause of that fearful condition of worldliness, backsliding, and spiritual death which existed in the churches in 1844. (ibid., 379-380)

Many of the Protestant churches are following Rome's example of iniquitous connection with "the kings of the earth"—the state churches, by their relation to secular governments; and other denominations, by seeking the favor of the world. And the term "Babylon"—confusion—may be appropriately applied to these bodies, all professing to derive their doctrines from the Bible, yet divided into almost innumerable sects, with widely conflicting creeds and theories. (ibid., 383)

Thus the stage was set for the abomination that causes desolation to be repeated in the great second advent movement.

> Christ had opened the door, or ministration, of the most holy place, light was shining from that open door of the sanctuary in heaven, and the fourth commandment was shown to be included in the law which is there enshrined; what God had established, no man could overthrow. (ibid., 435)
>
> Concerning the Sabbath, the Lord says, further, that it is "a sign, . . . that ye may know that I am the Lord your God." Ezekiel 20:20. And the reason given is: "For in six days the Lord made heaven and earth, and on the seventh day He rested, and was refreshed." Exodus 31:17.
>
> "The importance of the Sabbath as the memorial of creation is that it keeps ever present the true reason why worship is due to God"—because He is the Creator, and we are His creatures . . . . J. N. Andrews, *History of the Sabbath*, chapter 27. (ibid., 437)

Even with this clear instruction in the Bible concerning the sacred character of the Sabbath, the whole world is setting aside the law of God, more especially the Sabbath commandment.

> No error accepted by the Christian world strikes more boldly against the authority of Heaven, none is more directly opposed to the dictates of reason, none is more pernicious in its results, than the modern doctrine, so rapidly gaining ground, that God's law is no longer binding upon men. (ibid., 584)
>
> Already the doctrine that men are released from obedience to God's requirements has weakened the force of moral obligation and opened the floodgates of iniquity upon the world. Lawlessness, dissipation, and corruption are sweeping in upon us like an overwhelming tide. (ibid., 585)
>
> [In the coming conflict] those who honor the Bible Sabbath will be denounced as enemies of law and order, as breaking down the moral restraints of society, causing anarchy and

corruption, and calling down the judgments of God upon the earth. Their conscientious scruples will be pronounced obstinacy, stubbornness, and contempt of authority. They will be accused of disaffection toward the government. Ministers who deny the obligation of the divine law will present from the pulpit the duty of yielding obedience to the civil authorities as ordained of God. In legislative halls and courts of justice, commandment keepers will be misrepresented and condemned. A false coloring will be given to their words; the worst construction will be put upon their motives.

As the Protestant churches reject the clear, Scriptural arguments in defense of God's law, they will long to silence those whose faith they cannot overthrow by the Bible. Though they blind their own eyes to the fact, they are now adopting a course which will lead to the persecution of those who conscientiously refuse to do what the rest of the Christian world are doing, and acknowledge the claims of the papal sabbath.

The dignitaries of church and state will unite to bribe, persuade, or compel all classes to honor the Sunday. The lack of divine authority will be supplied by oppressive enactments. Political corruption is destroying love of justice and regard for truth; and even in free America, rulers and legislators, in order to secure public favor, will yield to the popular demand for a law enforcing Sunday observance. Liberty of conscience, which has cost so great a sacrifice, will no longer be respected. In the soon-coming conflict we shall see exemplified the prophet's words: "The dragon was wroth with the woman, and went to make war with the remnant of her seed, which keep the commandments of God, and have the testimony of Jesus Christ." Revelation 12:17. (ibid., 592)

In the first advent of Christ, a similar rejection of truth existed. As Christ was making His triumphal entry into Jerusalem just a few days before His crucifixion, as He reached the brow of the hill, the procession halted.

Before them lay Jerusalem in its glory, now bathed in the light of the declining sun. The temple attracted all eyes . . . .

Jesus gazes upon the scene, and the vast multitude hush their shouts, spellbound by the sudden vision of beauty. All eyes turn upon the Saviour, expecting to see in His countenance the admiration they themselves feel. But instead of this they behold a cloud of sorrow. They are surprised and disappointed to see His eyes fill with tears, and His body rock to and fro like a tree before the tempest, while a wail of anguish bursts from His quivering lips, as if from the depths of a broken heart. (*The Desire of Ages*, 575)

Christ came to save Jerusalem with her children; but Pharisaical pride, hypocrisy, jealousy, and malice had prevented Him from accomplishing His purpose. Jesus knew the terrible retribution which would be visited upon the doomed city. He saw Jerusalem encompassed with armies, the besieged inhabitants driven to starvation and death . . . . He saw the wretched inhabitants suffering torture on the rack and by crucifixion, the beautiful palaces destroyed, the temple in ruins, and of its massive walls not one stone left upon another, while the city was plowed like a field. Well might the Saviour weep in agony in view of that fearful scene.

Jerusalem had been the child of His care, and as a tender father mourns over a wayward son, so Jesus wept over the beloved city. How can I give thee up? How can I see thee devoted to destruction? Must I let thee go to fill up the cup of thine iniquity? One soul is of such value that, in comparison with it, worlds sink into insignificance; but here was a whole nation to be lost. When the fast westering sun should pass from sight in the heavens, Jerusalem's day of grace would be ended. (ibid., 577-578)

Christ saw in Jerusalem a symbol of the world hardened in unbelief and rebellion, and hastening on to meet the retributive judgments of God. The woes of a fallen race, pressing upon His soul, forced from His lips that exceeding bitter cry. He saw the record of sin traced in human misery, tears, and blood; His heart was moved with infinite pity for the afflicted and suffering ones of earth; He yearned to relieve them all. But even His hand might not turn back the tide of human woe; few would seek their only source of help. He was willing to pour out His soul unto death, to bring salvation within their reach; but few would come to Him that they might have life.

The Majesty of heaven in tears! The Son of the infinite God troubled in spirit, bowed down with anguish! The scene filled all heaven with wonder. That scene reveals to us the exceeding sinfulness of sin; it shows how hard a task it is, even for Infinite Power, to save the guilty from the consequences of transgressing the law of God. Jesus, looking down to the last generation, saw the world involved in a deception similar to that which caused the destruction of Jerusalem. The great sin of the Jews was their rejection of Christ; the great sin of the Christian world would be their rejection of the law of God, the foundation of His government in heaven and earth. The precepts of Jehovah would be despised and set at nought. Millions in bondage to sin, slaves of Satan, doomed to suffer the second death, would refuse to listen to the words of truth in their day of visitation. Terrible blindness! strange infatuation! (*The Great Controversy*, 22-23)

In the closing scenes of the controversy,

The Sabbath will be the great test of loyalty, for it is the point of truth especially controverted. When the final test shall be brought to bear upon men, then the line of distinction will be drawn between those who serve God and those who serve Him not. While the observance of the false sabbath in compliance with the law of the state, contrary to the fourth commandment, will be an avowal of allegiance to a power that is in opposition to God, the keeping of the true Sabbath, in obedience to God's law, is an evidence of loyalty to the Creator. While one class, by accepting the sign of submission to earthly powers, receive the mark of the beast [Rev. 14:10, 11], the other choosing the token of allegiance to divine authority, receive the seal of God. (ibid., 605)

Fearful is the issue to which the world is to be brought. The powers of earth, uniting to war against the commandments of God, will decree that "all, both small and great, rich and poor, free and bond" (Revelation 13:16), shall conform to the customs of the church by the observance of the false sabbath.

All who refuse compliance will be visited with civil penalties, and it will finally be declared that they are deserving of death. (ibid., 604)

As the controversy extends into new fields and the minds of the people are called to God's downtrodden law, Satan is astir. The power attending the message will only madden those who oppose it. The clergy will put forth almost superhuman efforts to shut away the light lest it should shine upon their flocks. By every means at their command they will endeavor to suppress the discussion of these vital questions. The church appeals to the strong arm of civil power, and, in this work, papists and Protestants unite. As the movement for Sunday enforcement becomes more bold and decided, the law will be invoked against commandment keepers. They will be threatened with fines and imprisonment, and some will be offered positions of influence, and other rewards and advantages, as inducements to renounce their faith. (ibid., 607)

To human wisdom all this now seems impossible; but as the restraining Spirit of God shall be withdrawn from men, and they shall be under the control of Satan, who hates the divine precepts, there will be strange developments. (ibid., 608)

We are nearing the close of this earth's history. Satan is making desperate efforts to make himself god, to speak and act like God, to appear as one who has a right to control the consciences of men. He strives with all his power to place a human institution in the position of God's holy rest-day. Under the jurisdiction of the man of sin, men have exalted a false standard in complete opposition to God's enactment. Each Sabbath institution bears the name of its author, an ineffaceable mark showing the authority of each. The first day of the week has not one particle of sanctity. It is the production of the man of sin, who strives in this way to counterwork God's purposes. (*The Review and Herald*, April 23, 1901)

The Protestants of the United States will be foremost in stretching their hands across the gulf to grasp the hand of spiritualism; they will reach over the abyss to clasp hands with the Roman power; and under the influence of this threefold union, this country will follow in the steps of Rome in trampling on the rights of conscience.

As spiritualism more closely imitates the nominal Christianity of the day, it has greater power to deceive and ensnare. Satan himself is converted, after the modern order of things. He will appear in the character of an angel of light. Through the agency of spiritualism, miracles will be wrought, the sick will be healed, and many undeniable wonders will be performed. (*The Great Controversy*, 588)

As the crowning act in the great drama of deception, Satan himself will personate Christ. The church has long professed to look to the Saviour's advent as the consummation of her hopes. Now the great deceiver will make it appear that Christ has come. In different parts of the earth, Satan will manifest himself among men as a majestic being of dazzling brightness, resembling the description of the Son of God given by John in the Revelation. Revelation 1:13-15. The glory that surrounds him is unsurpassed by anything that mortal eyes have yet beheld. The shout of triumph rings out upon the air: "Christ has come! Christ has come!" The people prostrate themselves in adoration before him, while he lifts up his hands and pronounces a blessing upon them, as Christ blessed His disciples when He was upon the earth. His voice is soft and subdued, yet full of melody. In gentle, compassionate tones he presents some of the same gracious, heavenly truths which the Saviour uttered; he heals the diseases of the people, and then, in his assumed character of Christ, he claims to have changed the Sabbath to Sunday, and commands all to hallow the day which he has blessed. He declares that those who persist in keeping holy the seventh day are blaspheming his name by refusing to listen to his angels sent to them with light and truth. This is the strong, almost overmastering delusion. (ibid., 624)

In Satan's personation of Christ and his public stand against Christ and the law of God, we see the fulfillment of Daniel 8:25, "He will destroy many and take his stand against the Prince of princes."

Thus the distinction is drawn between the loyal and the disloyal. Those who desire to have the seal of God in their foreheads must keep the Sabbath of the Fourth Commandment. Thus they are distinguished from the disloyal, who have accepted a man-made institution in place of the true Sabbath. The observance of God's rest-day is a mark of distinction between him that serveth God and him that serveth Him not.

When men make the assertion that a change has been made in the law of God's government, they cast a reflection upon God's character. If the law was just when given to Adam, it is just today. "It is easier for heaven and earth to pass," Christ declared, "than one tittle of the law to fail."

The substitution of the false for the true is the last act in the drama. When this substitution becomes universal, God will reveal himself. When the laws of men are exalted above the laws of God, when the powers of this earth try to force men to keep the first day of the week, know that the time has come for God to work. He will arise in His majesty, and will shake terribly the earth. He will come out of His place to punish the inhabitants of the world for their iniquity. The earth shall disclose her blood, and shall no more cover her slain.

The belief that the law of God is not the standard of righteousness is now almost universal in the Christian world. Professed Christians think that the more contempt they place upon the law, the more commendable they are in God's sight. Each human being exerts an influence upon those with whom he associates. Those who are willing to be led by false theories and unsound doctrines, who build their hopes for eternity on shifting sand, will find that the storm and tempest of trial will sweep away their refuge of lies. Their structure will fall, and they will perish,—lost, lost for all eternity. (*The Review and Herald*, April 23, 1901)

In his final struggle in the controversy with Christ over the law of God, Satan again develops an abomination that causes astounding devastation.

The coming conflict is described as a whole world rebelling against the law of God, which is the transcript of His character and the standard in the judgment. There will be a grand movement to do away with the law of God and replace it with the traditions of the church.

Without this standard in the judgment, there is no need for the atoning blood of Christ to cover the confessed sin of the repentant sinner for where there is no law there is no transgression. Romans 4:15. Without the need of the atoning blood of Jesus in the sanctuary in heaven, there is no need for Jesus to have died on the cross. Thus the ministry of Jesus in the most holy place of the sanctuary in heaven and the great plan of salvation is completely destroyed in the minds of the people by this abominable teaching that there is no law.

The abomination that causes desolation—the attempt to destroy God's law and the knowledge of Christ's final ministry in the most holy place of the heavenly sanctuary where the great original of God's law is located—will be repeated.

> But the people of God will not be misled. The teachings of this false christ are not in accordance with the Scriptures. His blessing is pronounced upon the worshipers of the beast and his image, the very class upon whom the Bible declares that God's unmingled wrath shall be poured out. (*The Great Controversy*, 625)

During this final struggle, the foundation and central message of the people of God will be the atoning ministry of Christ in the most holy place of the sanctuary in heaven.

> The great work of the gospel is not to close with less manifestation of the power of God than marked its opening. The prophecies which were fulfilled in the outpouring of the former rain at the opening of the gospel are again to be fulfilled in the latter rain at its close. Here are "the times of refreshing" to which the apostle Peter looked forward when he said: "Repent ye therefore, and be converted, that your sins may be blotted out, when the times of refreshing shall come from the presence of the Lord; and He shall send Jesus." Acts 3:19, 20. (ibid., 611-612)

In the midst of this great abomination that causes desolation, shines the light from the most holy place, and a voice is heard saying, "Come to me, all you who are weary and burdened, and I will give you rest." "To him who is thirsty I will give to drink without cost from the spring of the water of life. He who overcomes will inherit all this, and I will be his God and he will be my son." (Matt. 11:28; Rev. 21:6-7)

Closing Events Time Line

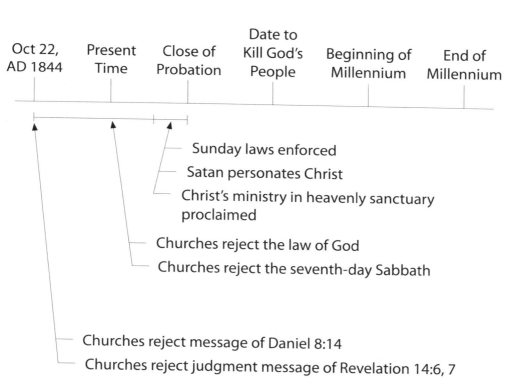

| Oct 22, AD 1844 | Present Time | Close of Probation | Date to Kill God's People | Beginning of Millennium | End of Millennium |

— Sunday laws enforced

— Satan personates Christ

— Christ's ministry in heavenly sanctuary proclaimed

— Churches reject the law of God

— Churches reject the seventh-day Sabbath

— Churches reject message of Daniel 8:14

— Churches reject judgment message of Revelation 14:6, 7

13

The Restoration of the
Kingdom of Glory Begins

In chapter 2 we noted that with the fall of Adam and Eve and the institution of the plan of salvation, the kingdom of glory was immediately replaced by the kingdom of grace. We are now in the time of the closing events of the great controversy between Christ and Satan. It is during this time that God begins the process of restoring the kingdom of glory. At the beginning of the controversy, the government of heaven was very quickly changed from the kingdom of glory to the kingdom of grace. But in the closing work, we will find that the restoration of the kingdom of glory will take over 1,000 years. In this chapter, we will begin the study of the events involved in the process of restoring the kingdom of glory.

Jesus Himself announced the time for the great second advent movement to begin. John describes the scene in Revelation 10.

> Then I saw another mighty angel coming down from heaven. He was robed in a cloud, with a rainbow above his head; his face was like the sun, and his legs were like fiery pillars. He was holding a little scroll, which lay open in his hand. He planted his right foot on the sea and his left foot on the land, and he gave a loud shout like the roar of a lion.
>
> Then the angel I had seen standing on the sea and on the land raised his right hand to heaven. And he swore by him who lives for ever and ever, who created the heavens and all that is in them, the earth and all that is in it, and the sea and all that is in it, and said, "There will be no more delay! But in the days when the seventh angel is about to sound his trumpet, the mystery of God will be accomplished, just as he announced to his servants the prophets." (Rev. 10:1-3, 5-7)

Christ says that when the seventh trumpet begins to sound, "the mystery of God will be accomplished, just as he announced to his servants the prophets." In chapter 11, we studied the seventh trumpet from the viewpoint of Jesus working as our high priest and mediator. But there is another phase of work that Jesus began on October 22, 1844, in the most holy place, which is brought to light in the seventh trumpet.

Two times it mentions the reign of Jesus.

> The kingdom of the world has become the kingdom of our Lord and of his Christ, and he will *reign* for ever and ever. You have taken your great power and have begun to *reign*.
> (Rev 11:15, 17) (Emphasis supplied.)

We know from our study in chapter 11 that the seventh trumpet began to sound on October 22, 1844, therefore His reign began on this date also. This reign cannot refer to Jesus in His role as our high priest and mediator—the Lamb of God. In His role as a mediator and servant, He wears the garments of a priest. His work as our high priest and mediator ends at the close of probation; it does not go on forever and ever as it says it will do when He begins His reign as a king.

This reign must be understood in the light of the beginning of the restoration of the kingdom of glory. On October 22, 1844, Jesus began to determine who will be the subjects of His kingdom of glory. This is clearly taught by the parable of the wedding banquet in Matthew 22. This is not the work of a mediator, but that of a king. The determination of who will be accepted into the kingdom of glory is the first step in the restoration of the kingdom of glory. It is in this sense that Jesus began to reign on October 22, 1844.

The weight of evidence shows that during the time of the investigative judgment, which began on October 22, 1844, Jesus functions in two capacities—(1) as a high priest and mediator, pleading His blood in behalf of sinners, and (2) as a king determining who will be the subjects of His soon-to-be-established kingdom of glory. Jesus is completing His last phase of work as a high priest and mediator under the kingdom of grace and beginning his first phase of work as a reigning king under the kingdom of glory. In these two functions taking place at the same time, we see the beginning of the transition of the government of heaven from the kingdom of grace back to the kingdom of glory.

The parable of the ten virgins (Matt. 25:1-13) is a description of the church during the great second advent movement. The first few verses represent the church before October 22, 1844.

> At that time the kingdom of heaven will be like ten virgins who took their lamps and went out to meet the bridegroom. Five of them were foolish and five were wise. The foolish ones took their lamps but did not take any oil with them. The wise, however, took oil in jars along with their lamps. The bridegroom was a long time in coming, and they all became drowsy and fell asleep. (Matt. 25:1-5)

Verse 5 says that all the virgins fell asleep. This sleep of the virgins represents spiritual insensitivity. They had not kept up with the light of truth, which the Lord desired to give them. When the message that the sanctuary was to be restored was proclaimed, prior to 1844, all of the churches thought that the earth was the sanctuary. The churches, represented by the sleeping virgins, were all spiritually asleep concerning this point of truth. These first five verses cannot apply after October 22, 1844, because there is no evidence that all the virgins fell asleep on any one point of doctrine after this date as they did on the mistaken belief that the earth was the sanctuary.

When the message, "Behold, the bridegroom cometh; go ye out to meet him" (Matt. 25:6, KJV) was proclaimed, everyone expected Jesus to come to this earth on October 22, 1844. When Jesus did not appear on earth, there was a great disappointment, and many professed believers left the advent movement, never to return.

The bridegroom did come at that time, but not to this earth. He came to the Ancient of Days (Dan. 7:9-10, 13) to begin the work of determining who would be the subjects of the kingdom of glory.

> The proclamation, "Behold, the Bridegroom cometh," in the summer of 1844, led thousands to expect the immediate advent of the Lord. At the appointed time the Bridegroom came, not to the earth, as the people expected, but to the Ancient of Days in heaven, to the marriage, the reception of His kingdom. "They that were ready went in with Him to the marriage: and the door was shut." They were not to be present in person at the marriage; for it takes place in heaven, while they are upon

the earth. The followers of Christ are to "wait for their Lord, when He will *return from* the wedding." Luke 12:36. But they are to understand His work, and to follow Him by faith as He goes in before God. It is in this sense that they are said to go in to the marriage. (*The Great Controversy*, 427)

In the parable of Matthew 22 the same figure of the marriage is introduced, and the investigative judgment is clearly represented as taking place before the marriage. Previous to the wedding the king comes in to see the guests, to see if all are attired in the wedding garment, the spotless robe of character washed and made white in the blood of the Lamb. Matthew 22:11; Revelation 7:14. He who is found wanting is cast out, but all who upon examination are seen to have the wedding garment on are accepted of God and accounted worthy of a share in His kingdom and a seat upon His throne. This work of examination of character, of determining who are prepared for the kingdom of God, is that of the investigative judgment, the closing work in the sanctuary above. (ibid., 428)

When Jesus was talking with His disciples, He explained that there would be a transition from the kingdom of grace back to the kingdom of glory and He told them when it would occur. He said,

> "When the Son of man shall come in His glory, and all the holy angels with Him, then shall He sit upon the throne of His glory: and before Him shall be gathered all nations." Matthew 25:31, 32. This kingdom is yet future. It is not to be set up until the second advent of Christ. (ibid., 347)

This transition of government is further explained in the following reference:

> He "shall sit and rule upon His throne; and He shall be a priest upon His throne." Not now "upon the throne of His glory;" the kingdom of glory has not yet been ushered in. Not until His work as a mediator shall be ended will God "give unto Him the throne of His father David," a kingdom of which "there shall be no end." Luke 1:32, 33. As a priest, Christ is

now set down with the Father in His throne. Revelation 3:21. (ibid., 416)

"And, behold, one like the Son of man came with the clouds of heaven, and came to the Ancient of Days, and they brought Him near before Him. And there was given Him dominion, and glory, and a kingdom, that all people, nations, and languages, should serve Him: His dominion is an everlasting dominion, which shall not pass away." Daniel 7:13, 14. The coming of Christ here described is not His second coming to the earth. He comes to the Ancient of Days in heaven to receive dominion and glory and a kingdom, which will be given Him at the close of His work as a mediator. It is this coming, and not His second advent to the earth, that was foretold in prophecy to take place at the termination of the 2300 days in 1844. Attended by heavenly angels, our great High Priest enters the holy of holies and there appears in the presence of God to engage in the last acts of His ministration in behalf of man—to perform the work of investigative judgment and to make an atonement for all who are shown to be entitled to its benefits. (ibid., 479-480)

In this information, we have a clear picture presented of the dual role of Jesus in the heavenly sanctuary between October 22, 1844, and the close of probation. On the one hand, Jesus is still functioning as a high priest and mediator, receiving those who come to Him with their burden of sin to be washed away in the blood of the Lamb. On the other hand, He is working as a king, determining who will be His subjects in the coming kingdom of glory. The time is just before us when probation will close.

Then Jesus ceases His intercession in the sanctuary above. He lifts His hands and with a loud voice says, "It is done;" and all the angelic host lay off their crowns as He makes the solemn announcement: "He that is unjust, let him be unjust still: and he which is filthy, let him be filthy still: and he that is righteous, let him be righteous still: and he that is holy, let him be holy still." Revelation 22:11. Every case has been decided for life or death. Christ has made the atonement for His people and blotted out their sins. The number of His subjects is made up; "the kingdom and dominion, and the greatness of the kingdom under the whole heaven," is about to be given to the heirs of salvation, and Jesus is to reign as King of kings and Lord of lords. (ibid., 613-614)

Dear friend, are you making your plans to become a subject of the coming kingdom of glory? Jesus is sending you this final invitation.

> To him who is thirsty I will give to drink without cost from the spring of the water of life. He who overcomes will inherit all this, and I will be his God and he will be my son. (Rev. 21:6-7)

Closing Events Time Line

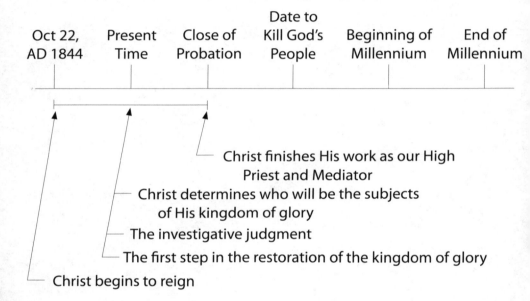

14

The Wedding of the Lamb

> After this I heard what sounded like the roar of a great multitude in heaven shouting: "Hallelujah! Salvation and glory and power belong to our God, for true and just are his judgments. He has condemned the great prostitute who corrupted the earth by her adulteries. He has avenged on her the blood of his servants."
>
> —Revelation 19:1-2

When the investigative judgment ends, there is great rejoicing in heaven. God the Father and Christ have completed the first step in the restoration of the kingdom of glory. They have determined who from this earth will be the subjects of the kingdom of glory. They have also condemned the great prostitute (Babylon) for corrupting the earth with her adulteries. *Adulteries* is a biblical term that symbolizes false teachings or false doctrines.

> And again they shouted: "Hallelujah! The smoke from her goes up for ever and ever." The twenty-four elders and the four living creatures fell down and worshiped God, who was seated on the throne. And they cried: "Amen, Hallelujah!" Then a voice came from the throne, saying: "Praise our God, all you his servants, you who fear him, both small and great!"
>
> Then I heard what sounded like a great multitude, like the roar of rushing waters and like loud peals of thunder, shouting: "Hallelujah! For our Lord God Almighty reigns. Let us rejoice and be glad and give him glory! For the wedding of the Lamb has come, and his bride has made herself ready." (Rev. 19:3-7)

What is the wedding of the Lamb? When do preparations for the wedding begin? When does the wedding take place? Where is it held? What is the purpose of the wedding? Who is the bride?

In the previous chapter, we found that Matthew 25:1-13—the parable of the ten virgins—is a description of the second advent movement during which Christ begins to bring the reign of sin to a close and to restore the kingdom of glory that was interrupted by rebellion against God and His holy and righteous law. The announcement was made in Matthew 25:6, "Here's the bridegroom! Come out to meet him!" This message was first given in the summer of 1844.

> The coming of the bridegroom, here brought to view, takes place before the marriage. The marriage represents the reception by Christ of His kingdom. (*The Great Controversy*, 426)

The kingdom that Christ receives is the kingdom of glory, which will never end (Rev. 11:15). At the wedding of the Lamb, Christ will receive authority as "King of kings" over His kingdom—the kingdom of glory. As described in the previous chapter, Christ came to the marriage in 1844, not to this earth as the people expected, but to the Ancient of Days to examine the records in order to determine who will be the subjects of His eternal kingdom. This process, referred to as the investigative judgment, is in progress at the present time. Christ has begun His work to restore the kingdom of glory to its original condition before the fall of Adam and Eve.

The change in Christ's ministration is explained in the following quotation.

> He "shall sit and rule upon His throne; and He shall be a priest upon His throne." Not now "upon the throne of His glory;" the kingdom of glory has not yet been ushered in. Not until His work as a mediator shall be ended will God "give unto Him the throne of His father David," a kingdom of which "there shall be no end." Luke 1:32, 33. (ibid., 416)

When the announcement is made, "Let him who does wrong continue to do wrong; let him who is vile continue to be vile; let him who does right continue to do right; and let him who is holy continue to be holy" (Rev. 22:11), probation for mankind closes, the sanctuary in heaven closes, and the kingdom of grace comes to an end. There is great rejoicing in heaven and immediately preparations are made for the wedding of the Lamb.

> "He shall bear the glory." To Christ belongs the glory of redemption for the fallen race. Through the eternal ages, the song of the ransomed ones will be: "Unto Him that loved us, and washed us from our sins in His own blood, . . . to Him be glory and dominion for ever and ever." Revelation 1:5, 6. (ibid., 416)

When Christ finishes His work as mediator, then will be given to "him the throne of his father David, and he will reign over the house of Jacob forever; his kingdom [of glory] will never end" (Luke 1:32-33). At this wedding,

> The Holy City, the New Jerusalem, which is the capital and representative of the kingdom, is called "the bride, the Lamb's wife." Said the angel to John: "Come hither, I will show thee the bride, the Lamb's wife." . . . "He carried me away in the spirit," says the prophet, "and showed me that great city, the holy Jerusalem, descending out of heaven from God." Revelation 21:9, 10. (ibid., 426, 427)

At this point, we need to examine the teaching that says that the church is the bride of Christ. These two doctrines—(1) that the church is the bride and (2) that the New Jerusalem is the bride—would appear to be in direct conflict, but that is not the case. When correctly understood in their proper settings, they are in perfect harmony.

We learned in chapter 2 that at the fall of Adam and Eve, the kingdom of glory came to an immediate end, and the kingdom of grace was set up in its place. The kingdom of grace was to continue to the close of probation—the close of Christ's ministry in the sanctuary in heaven. It is in the kingdom of grace that the church is referred to as "the bride." Many texts both in the Old Testament and in the New Testament refer to the church, the people of God, as a bride. Under the kingdom of grace, Christ uses this representation to express His great love for His people, and He uses this human relationship to convey this thought to them. There are no biblical references to a wedding during the kingdom of grace.

The question we need to ask is, since the Holy City, the New
Jerusalem, is the "bride, the Lamb's wife," what part does the church
have at this wedding? The disciple John says,

> "Blessed are those who are invited to the wedding supper
> of the Lamb!" And he added, "These are the true words of
> God." (Rev. 19:9)

John represents them as "guests" at the wedding supper. This is
in harmony with the parable Jesus gave in Matthew 22 where the
king examined the guests to see who had the wedding garment on
for the wedding banquet. The following statement explains it quite
clearly.

> In the Revelation the people of God are said to be the
> guests at the marriage supper. Revelation 19:9. If *guests*, they
> cannot be represented also as the *bride*. Christ, as stated by the
> prophet Daniel, will receive from the Ancient of Days in heaven,
> "dominion, and glory, and a kingdom;" He will receive the New
> Jerusalem, the capital of His kingdom, "prepared as a bride
> adorned for her husband." Daniel 7:14; Revelation 21:2. Having
> received the kingdom, He will come in His glory, as King of
> kings and Lord of lords, for the redemption of His people, who
> are to "sit down with Abraham, and Isaac, and Jacob," at His
> table in His kingdom (Matthew 8:11; Luke 22:30), to partake
> of the marriage supper of the Lamb.
>
> The proclamation, "Behold, the Bridegroom cometh," in
> the summer of 1844, led thousands to expect the immediate
> advent of the Lord. At the appointed time the Bridegroom came,
> not to the earth, as the people expected, but to the Ancient of
> Days in heaven, to the marriage, the reception of His kingdom.
> "They that were ready went in with Him to the marriage: and
> the door was shut." They were not to be present in person at
> the marriage; for it takes place in heaven, while they are upon
> the earth. The followers of Christ are to "wait for their Lord,
> when He will *return from* the wedding." Luke 12:36. But they
> are to understand His work, and to follow Him by faith as He
> goes in before God. It is in this sense that they are said to go
> in to the marriage. (ibid., 427)

It is at this wedding, which takes place soon after the close of probation, that Jesus receives His crown of authority as "King of kings" and "Lord of lords" over the kingdom of glory. It is at the second coming of Jesus that Christ will take the subjects of His kingdom from this earth to be with Him in the kingdom of glory.

The opening text in this chapter—Revelation 19:2—says that the great prostitute has been condemned. When this pronouncement is made, the ministry of Christ in the heavenly sanctuary is completed and probation is closed—"the door was shut" (Matt. 25:10). The wedding of the Lamb spoken of in Revelation 19:7 is the second step in the process of restoring the kingdom of glory back to its original state.

The time of the wedding of the Lamb is identified on the time line below.

Closing Events Time Line

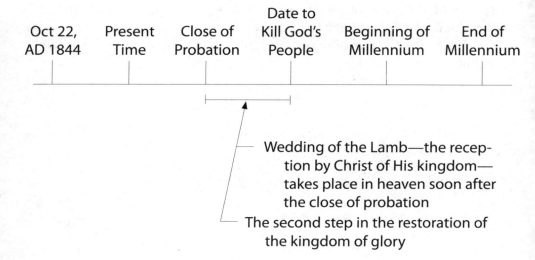

Oct 22, AD 1844	Present Time	Close of Probation	Date to Kill God's People	Beginning of Millennium	End of Millennium

Wedding of the Lamb—the reception by Christ of His kingdom—takes place in heaven soon after the close of probation

The second step in the restoration of the kingdom of glory

15

The Time of Jacob's Trouble

While the marriage is taking place in heaven, what is happening on the earth, where the people of God—the subjects of the kingdom of glory—are still being held captive by Satan and his followers? No one on earth will know when the time passes when their eternal destiny is forever settled.

> The forms of religion will be continued by a people from whom the Spirit of God has been finally withdrawn; and the satanic zeal with which the prince of evil will inspire them for the accomplishment of his malignant designs, will bear the semblance of zeal for God. (*The Great Controversy*, 615)

Although the forms of religion do not change when probation closes, the environment on earth begins to change very rapidly.

> When Christ ceases His intercession in the sanctuary, the unmingled wrath threatened against those who worship the beast and his image and receive his mark (Revelation 14:9, 10), will be poured out . . . . Says the revelator, in describing those terrific scourges: "There fell a noisome and grievous sore upon the men which had the mark of the beast, and upon them which worshiped his image." The sea "became as the blood of a dead man: and every living soul died in the sea." And "the rivers and fountains of waters . . . became blood." Terrible as these inflictions are, God's justice stands fully vindicated. The angel of God declares: "Thou art righteous, O Lord, . . . because Thou hast judged thus. For they have shed the blood of saints and prophets, and Thou hast given them blood to drink; for they are worthy." Revelation 16:2-6. By condemning the people of God

to death, they have as truly incurred the guilt of their blood as if it had been shed by their hands. In like manner Christ declared the Jews of His time guilty of all the blood of holy men which had been shed since the days of Abel; for they possessed the same spirit and were seeking to do the same work with these murderers of the prophets.

In the plague that follows, power is given to the sun "to scorch men with fire. And men were scorched with great heat." Verses 8, 9. (ibid., 627-628)

As soon as probation closes, the first four plagues recorded in Revelation 16 begin to fall upon the inhabitants of the earth.

> These plagues are not universal, or the inhabitants of the earth would be wholly cut off. Yet they will be the most awful scourges that have ever been known to mortals. All the judgments upon men, prior to the close of probation, have been mingled with mercy. The pleading blood of Christ has shielded the sinner from receiving the full measure of his guilt; but in the final judgment, wrath is poured out unmixed with mercy. (ibid., 628-629)

> Those who honor the law of God have been accused of bringing judgments upon the world, and they will be regarded as the cause of the fearful convulsions of nature and the strife and bloodshed among men that are filling the earth with woe. (ibid., 614)

> As the Sabbath has become the special point of controversy throughout Christendom, and religious and secular authorities have combined to enforce the observance of the Sunday, the persistent refusal of a small minority to yield to the popular demand will make them objects of universal execration. It will be urged that the few who stand in opposition to an institution of the church and a law of the state ought not to be tolerated; that it is better for them to suffer than for whole nations to be thrown into confusion and lawlessness. The same argument eighteen hundred years ago was brought against Christ by the rulers of the people . . . . This argument will appear conclusive. (ibid., 615)

The people conclude that if they kill all of the Sabbath keepers, these fearful judgments will be stopped, and normal conditions will again be restored to this earth. The churches go to the government leaders and plead for permission to slay the people of God, believing that in doing this these plagues will end.

> A decree will finally be issued against those who hallow the Sabbath of the fourth commandment, denouncing them as deserving of the severest punishment and giving the people liberty, after a certain time, to put them to death. Romanism in the Old World and apostate Protestantism in the New will pursue a similar course toward those who honor all the divine precepts. (ibid., 615-616)

When the world sets the date on which to kill all of the Sabbath keepers, "The people of God will then be plunged into those scenes of affliction and distress described by the prophet as the time of Jacob's trouble." (ibid., 616)

This is a fearful time for the little company who keep the commandments of God and who resist an institution of the church and a law of the state.

> As Satan accuses the people of God on account of their sins, the Lord permits him to try them to the uttermost. Their confidence in God, their faith and firmness, will be severely tested. As they review the past, their hopes sink; for in their whole lives they can see little good. They are fully conscious of their weakness and unworthiness. Satan endeavors to terrify them with the thought that their cases are hopeless, that the stain of their defilement will never be washed away. He hopes so to destroy their faith that they will yield to his temptations and turn from their allegiance to God.
>
> Though God's people will be surrounded by enemies who are bent upon their destruction, yet the anguish which they suffer is not a dread of persecution for the truth's sake; they fear that every sin has not been repented of, and that through some fault in themselves they will fail to realize the fulfillment of the Saviour's promise: I "will keep thee from the hour of temptation, which shall come upon all the world." Revelation 3:10.

On every hand they hear the plottings of treason and see the active working of rebellion; and there is aroused within them an intense desire, an earnest yearning of soul, that this great apostasy may be terminated and the wickedness of the wicked may come to an end. But while they plead with God to stay the work of rebellion, it is with a keen sense of self-reproach that they themselves have no more power to resist and urge back the mighty tide of evil. They feel that had they always employed all their ability in the service of Christ, going forward from strength to strength, Satan's forces would have less power to prevail against them.

They afflict their souls before God, pointing to their past repentance of their many sins, and pleading the Saviour's promise: "Let him take hold of My strength, that he may make peace with Me; and he shall make peace with Me." Isaiah 27:5. Their faith does not fail because their prayers are not immediately answered. Though suffering the keenest anxiety, terror, and distress, they do not cease their intercessions. They lay hold of the strength of God as Jacob laid hold of the Angel; and the language of their souls is: "I will not let Thee go, except Thou bless me." (ibid., 618-620)

All who will lay hold of God's promises, as he did, and be as earnest and persevering as he was, will succeed as he succeeded. (ibid., 621)

Says the psalmist: "In the time of trouble He shall hide me in His pavilion: in the secret of His tabernacle shall He hide me." Psalm 27:5. Christ has spoken: "Come, My people, enter thou into thy chambers, and shut thy doors about thee: hide thyself as it were for a little moment, until the indignation be overpast. For, behold, the Lord cometh out of His place to punish the inhabitants of the earth for their iniquity." Isaiah 26:20, 21. Glorious will be the deliverance of those who have patiently waited for His coming and whose names are written in the book of life. (ibid., 634)

Such will be the experience of God's people on this earth while the wedding of the Lamb is taking place in heaven. By faith, they believe that God will deliver them on the date that the world has set to slay them.

The major events presented in this chapter are listed on the time line below.

Closing Events Time Line

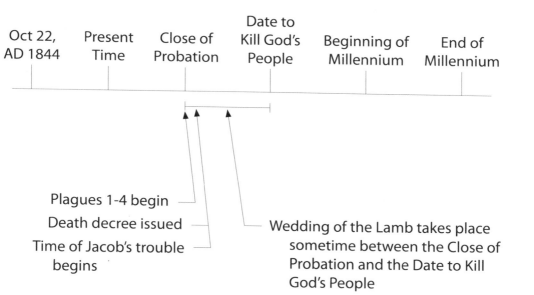

16

God Delivers His People

When the protection of human laws shall be withdrawn from those who honor the law of God, there will be, in different lands, a simultaneous movement for their destruction. As the time appointed in the decree draws near, the people will conspire to root out the hated sect. It will be determined to strike in one night a decisive blow, which shall utterly silence the voice of dissent and reproof.

The people of God—some in prison cells, some hidden in solitary retreats in the forests and the mountains—still plead for divine protection, while in every quarter companies of armed men, urged on by hosts of evil angels, are preparing for the work of death. It is now, in the hour of utmost extremity, that the God of Israel will interpose for the deliverance of His chosen. (*The Great Controversy*, 635)

The Lord says, "And you will sing as on the night you celebrate a holy festival; your hearts will rejoice as when people go up with flutes to the mountain of the LORD, to the Rock of Israel. The LORD will cause men to hear his majestic voice and will make them see his arm coming down with raging anger and consuming fire, with cloudburst, thunderstorm and hail." (Isa. 30:29-30)

With shouts of triumph, jeering, and imprecation, throngs of evil men are about to rush upon their prey, when, lo, a dense blackness, deeper than the darkness of the night, falls upon the earth. (ibid., 635-636)

This dense blackness falling upon the earth is a fulfillment of the fifth plague.

> The fifth angel poured out his bowl on the throne of the beast, and his kingdom was *plunged into darkness*. Men gnawed their tongues in agony and cursed the God of heaven because of their pains and their sores, but they refused to repent of what they had done. (Rev. 16:10-11) (Emphasis supplied.)

> Then a rainbow, shining with the glory from the throne of God, spans the heavens and seems to encircle each praying company. The angry multitudes are suddenly arrested. Their mocking cries die away. The objects of their murderous rage are forgotten. With fearful forebodings they gaze upon the symbol of God's covenant and long to be shielded from its overpowering brightness.

> By the people of God a voice, clear and melodious, is heard, saying, "Look up," and lifting their eyes to the heavens, they behold the bow of promise. The black, angry clouds that covered the firmament are parted, and like Stephen they look up steadfastly into heaven and see the glory of God and the Son of man seated upon His throne. In His divine form they discern the marks of His humiliation; and from His lips they hear the request presented before His Father and the holy angels: "I will that they also, whom Thou hast given Me, be with Me where I am." John 17:24. Again a voice, musical and triumphant, is heard, saying: "They come! they come! holy, harmless, and undefiled. They have kept the word of My patience; they shall walk among the angels;" and the pale, quivering lips of those who have held fast their faith utter a shout of victory.

> It is at midnight that God manifests His power for the deliverance of His people. The sun appears, shining in its strength. Signs and wonders follow in quick succession. The wicked look with terror and amazement upon the scene, while the righteous behold with solemn joy the tokens of their deliverance. Everything in nature seems turned out of its course. The streams cease to flow. Dark, heavy clouds come up and

clash against each other. In the midst of the angry heavens is one clear space of indescribable glory, whence comes the voice of God like the sound of many waters, saying: "It is done." Revelation 16:17. (ibid., 636)

This verse is quoted from the seventh plague (Rev. 16:17-21). Thus we see that the seventh plague also begins on the date that has been set to kill God's people.

That voice shakes the heavens and the earth. There is a mighty earthquake, "such as was not since men were upon the earth, so mighty an earthquake, and so great." Verses 17, 18. The firmament appears to open and shut. The glory from the throne of God seems flashing through. The mountains shake like a reed in the wind, and ragged rocks are scattered on every side. There is a roar as of a coming tempest. The sea is lashed into fury. There is heard the shriek of a hurricane like the voice of demons upon a mission of destruction. The whole earth heaves and swells like the waves of the sea. Its surface is breaking up. Its very foundations seem to be giving way. Mountain chains are sinking. Inhabited islands disappear. The seaports that have become like Sodom for wickedness are swallowed up by the angry waters. Babylon the great has come in remembrance before God, "to give unto her the cup of the wine of the fierceness of His wrath." Great hailstones, every one "about the weight of a talent," are doing their work of destruction. Verses 19, 21. (ibid., 636-637)

Several more verses from the seventh plague were quoted in the paragraph above, showing the terrible destruction of the earth that begins on the date to kill God's people. Verse 19 is of particular interest in that it makes reference to the fall of Babylon, which is the sixth plague (Rev. 16:12), as explained below.

"Her sins have reached unto heaven, and God hath remembered her iniquities . . . . In the cup which she hath filled fill to her double. How much she hath glorified herself, and lived deliciously, so much torment and sorrow give her: for she saith in her heart, I sit a queen, and am no widow, and shall see no sorrow. Therefore shall her plagues come in one day, death, and mourning, and famine; and she shall be utterly burned with fire: for strong is the Lord God who judgeth her. And the kings of the earth, who have committed fornication and lived deliciously with her, shall bewail her, and lament for her, . . . saying, Alas, alas that great city Babylon, that mighty city! for in one hour is thy judgment come." Revelation 18:5-10.

Such are the judgments that fall upon Babylon in the day of the visitation of God's wrath. She has filled up the measure of her iniquity; her time has come; she is ripe for destruction. (ibid., 653)

The subject of Revelation 18 is the fall of Babylon. This is the most complete description in the Bible of the sixth plague. This plague also begins on the date to kill God's people when the voice of God delivers them.

When the voice of God turns the captivity of His people, there is a terrible awakening of those who have lost all in the great conflict of life. While probation continued they were blinded by Satan's deceptions, and they justified their course of sin. The rich prided themselves upon their superiority to those who were less favored; but they had obtained their riches by violation of the law of God. They had neglected to feed the hungry, to clothe the naked, to deal justly, and to love mercy. They had sought to exalt themselves and to obtain the homage of their fellow creatures. Now they are stripped of all that made them great and are left destitute and defenseless. They look with terror upon the destruction of the idols which they preferred before their Maker. They have sold their souls for earthly riches and enjoyments, and have not sought to become rich toward God. The result is, their lives are a failure; their pleasures are now turned to gall, their treasures to corruption. The gain of a lifetime is swept away in a moment. The rich bemoan the destruction of their grand houses, the scattering of their gold and silver. But their lamentations are silenced by the fear that they themselves are to perish with their idols. (ibid., 654)

Ministers and people see that they have not sustained the right relation to God. They see that they have rebelled against the Author of all just and righteous law. The setting aside of the divine precepts gave rise to thousands of springs of evil, discord, hatred, iniquity, until the earth became one vast field of strife, one sink of corruption. This is the view that now appears to those who rejected truth and chose to cherish error. No language can express the longing which the disobedient and disloyal feel for that which they have lost forever—eternal life. Men whom the world has worshiped for their talents and eloquence now see these things in their true light. They realize what they have forfeited by transgression, and they fall at the feet of those whose fidelity they have despised and derided, and confess that God has loved them.

The people see that they have been deluded. They accuse one another of having led them to destruction; but all unite in heaping their bitterest condemnation upon the ministers. Unfaithful pastors have prophesied smooth things; they have led their hearers to make void the law of God and to persecute those who would keep it holy. Now, in their despair, these teachers confess before the world their work of deception. The multitudes are filled with fury. "We are lost!" they cry, "and you are the cause of our ruin;" and they turn upon the false shepherds. The very ones that once admired them most will pronounce the most dreadful curses upon them. The very hands that once crowned them with laurels will be raised for their destruction. The swords which were to slay God's people are now employed to destroy their enemies. Everywhere there is strife and bloodshed. (ibid., 655-656)

In review, we have learned that the fifth, sixth, and seventh plagues—darkness over the seat of the beast and his kingdom, the fall of Babylon, and terrible signs and wonders in the heavens with utter destruction of the earth—all begin on the date that the world has set to wipe out the people of God. But God delivers His people "in the hour of utmost extremity" (ibid., 635).

In addition to the seven plagues that are now falling upon the earth, other events are also taking place. Soon after the people of God are delivered on the date the world has set to kill them, a special resurrection takes place. Concerning this event Daniel writes, "Multitudes who sleep in the dust of the earth will awake: some to everlasting life, others to shame and everlasting contempt." (Dan. 12:2)

All who have died in the faith of the third angel's message come forth from the tomb glorified, to hear God's covenant of peace with those who have kept His law. "They also which pierced Him" (Revelation 1:7), those that mocked and derided Christ's dying agonies, and the most violent opposers of His truth and His people, are raised to behold Him in His glory and to see the honor placed upon the loyal and obedient. (ibid., 637)

Signs and wonders appear in the heavens, one following another. One of these events—the display of the two tables of stone with the Ten Commandments written by the finger of God—attracts special attention.

Then there appears against the sky a hand holding two tables of stone folded together. Says the prophet: "The heavens shall declare His righteousness: for God is judge Himself." Psalm 50:6. That holy law, God's righteousness, that amid thunder and flame was proclaimed from Sinai as the guide of life, is now revealed to men as the rule of judgment. The hand opens the tables, and there are seen the precepts of the Decalogue, traced as with a pen of fire. The words are so plain that all can read them. Memory is aroused, the darkness of superstition and heresy is swept from every mind, and God's ten words, brief, comprehensive, and authoritative, are presented to the view of all the inhabitants of the earth.

It is impossible to describe the horror and despair of those who have trampled upon God's holy requirements. The Lord gave them His law; they might have compared their characters with it and learned their defects while there was yet opportunity for repentance and reform; but in order to secure the favor of the world, they set aside its precepts and taught others to transgress. They have endeavored to compel God's people to profane His Sabbath. Now they are condemned by that law which they have despised. With awful distinctness they see that they are without excuse. They chose whom they would serve and worship. "Then shall ye return, and discern between the righteous and the wicked, between him that serveth God and him that serveth Him not." Malachi 3:18. (ibid., 639-640)

Following this grand display of the eternal law of God,

> The voice of God is heard from heaven, declaring the
> day and hour of Jesus' coming, and delivering the everlasting
> covenant to His people. Like peals of loudest thunder His words
> roll through the earth. The Israel of God stand listening, with
> their eyes fixed upward. Their countenances are lighted up with
> His glory, and shine as did the face of Moses when he came
> down from Sinai. The wicked cannot look upon them. And
> when the blessing is pronounced on those who have honored
> God by keeping His Sabbath holy, there is a mighty shout of
> victory. (ibid., 640)

With greatest eagerness, the people of God search the heavens to catch the first glimpse of their coming King and Deliverer.

Below is the Closing Events Time Line showing the important events presented in this chapter.

Closing Events Time Line

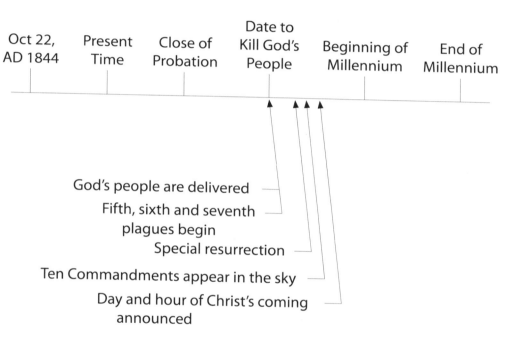

17

The Second Coming of Jesus to Fight the Battle of Armageddon

Whether the world is ready or not, the Lord Jesus Christ is going to return to this earth in the near future. The scriptures contain much information about this amazing event. It will not be a secret, for the Bible says, "Look, he is coming with the clouds, and every eye will see him, even those who pierced him; and all the peoples of the earth will mourn because of him" (Rev. 1:7). And all will hear Him, "For the Lord himself will come down from heaven, with a loud command, with the voice of the archangel and with the trumpet call of God" (1 Thess. 4:16).

While on the Isle of Patmos, the apostle John was given a vision of the second coming of Jesus. His description of the event is recorded in Revelation chapter 19. Beginning at verse 11, we read, "I saw heaven standing open and there before me was a white horse, whose rider is called Faithful and True. With justice he judges and makes war."

John uses a lot of symbolic language in his account. What do these symbols mean? Who is this rider? He is called "Faithful and True." Jesus Christ is the faithful witness (Rev. 1:5). Jesus is doing two things as He rides forth on His white horse. He is (1) judging and (2) making war. The concept of a war is further emphasized by the symbol of the horse that Jesus is riding. In the Bible, horses are nearly always seen in the setting of war. This horse is white, a symbol of purity (Isa. 1:18; Rev. 3:4-5). The symbolism used in Revelation 19:11 represents Jesus riding forth to fight a holy war.

Verses 12 and 13 further describe the rider on the white horse.

> His eyes are like blazing fire, and on his head are many crowns. He has a name written on him that no one knows but

he himself. He is dressed in a robe dipped in blood, and his name is the Word of God.

The many crowns indicate the great authority that Christ has received as King of the kingdom of glory.

The fact that He is dressed in a robe dipped in blood is very significant. An interesting reason for this unusual dress is found in the book of Isaiah.

> Who is this coming from Edom, from Bozrah, with his garments stained crimson? Who is this, robed in splendor, striding forward in the greatness of his strength? "It is I, [Christ] speaking in righteousness, mighty to save." Why are your garments red, like those of one treading the winepress? "I have trodden the winepress alone; from the nations no one was with me. I trampled them in my anger and trod them down in my wrath; their blood spattered my garments, and I stained all my clothing. For the day of vengeance was in my heart, and the year of my redemption has come. I looked, but there was no one to help, I was appalled that no one gave support; so my own arm worked salvation for me, and my own wrath sustained me. I trampled the nations in my anger; in my wrath I made them drunk and poured their blood on the ground."
>
> And blood flowed out of the press, rising as high as the horses' bridles for a distance of 1,600 stadia. (Isa. 63:1-6; Rev. 14:20)

Jesus is coming to bring justice and war upon those who have rejected His salvation and killed His saints. Jesus is not coming alone. "The armies of heaven were following him." (Rev. 19:14)

> With anthems of celestial melody the holy angels, a vast, unnumbered throng, attend Him on His way. The firmament seems filled with radiant forms—"ten thousand times ten thousand, and thousands of thousands." No human pen can portray the scene; no mortal mind is adequate to conceive its splendor. "His glory covered the heavens, and the earth was full of His praise. And His brightness was as the light."

Habakkuk 3:3, 4. As the living cloud comes still nearer, every eye beholds the Prince of life. (*The Great Controversy*, 641)

Out of his mouth comes a sharp sword with which to strike down the nations. (Rev. 19:15, last part)

For the word of God is living and active. Sharper than any double-edged sword, it penetrates even to dividing soul and spirit, joints and marrow; it judges the thoughts and attitudes of the heart. Nothing in all creation is hidden from God's sight. Everything is uncovered and laid bare before the eyes of him to whom we must give account. (Heb. 4:12, 13)

He will rule them with an iron scepter. (Rev. 19:15, middle part)

He treads the winepress of the fury of the wrath of God Almighty. (Rev. 19:15, last part)

When the great day of God's wrath comes,

The kings of the earth, the princes, the generals, the rich, the mighty, and every slave and every free man hid in caves and among the rocks of the mountains. They will call to the mountains and the rocks, "Fall on us and hide us from the face of him who sits on the throne and from the wrath of the Lamb! For the great day of their wrath has come, and who can stand?" (Rev. 6:15-17)

This is the time for the harvest of the earth.

I looked, and there before me was a white cloud, and seated on the cloud was one "like a son of man" with a crown of gold on his head and a sharp sickle in his hand. Then another angel came out of the temple and called in a loud voice to him who was sitting on the cloud, "Take your sickle and reap, because the time to reap has come, for the harvest of the earth is ripe." . . . Another angel came out of the temple in heaven, and he too had a sharp sickle. Still another angel . . . came from the altar and called in a loud voice to him who had the sharp sickle, "Take your sharp sickle and gather the clusters of grapes from the earth's vine, because its grapes are ripe." The angel swung his sickle on the earth, gathered its grapes and threw them into the great winepress of God's wrath. They were trampled in the winepress outside the city, and blood flowed out of the press, rising as high as the horses' bridles for a distance of 1,600 stadia. (Rev. 14:14-20)

The world has not been without warning of the great day of God's wrath. The third angel has been calling to the inhabitants of this earth since October 22, 1844, saying,

> If anyone worships the beast and his image and receives his mark on the forehead or on the hand, he, too, will drink of the wine of God's fury, which has been poured full strength into the cup of his wrath. He will be tormented with burning sulfur in the presence of the holy angels and of the Lamb . . . . There is no rest day or night for those who worship the beast and his image, or for anyone who receives the mark of his name. (Rev. 14:9-11)

The rider on the white horse—Jesus Christ—comes with the armies of heaven following Him.

> On his robe and on his thigh he has this name written: KING OF KINGS AND LORD OF LORDS. (Rev. 19:16)

At the wedding of the Lamb, when Jesus is given authority and dominion over the kingdom of glory, He will receive the title, "King of kings and Lord of lords."

As this wonderful scene is passing before his eyes, John writes,

> Then I saw the beast and the kings of the earth and their armies gathered together to make war against the rider on the horse and his army. (Rev. 19:19)

This is not a surprise battle for the beast and the kings of the earth. Preparations for this battle have been in progress for some time. The Revelator says,

> I saw three evil spirits that looked like frogs; they came out of the mouth of the dragon, out of the mouth of the beast

and out of the mouth of the false prophet . . . . They go out to
the kings of the whole world, to gather them for the battle on
the great day of God Almighty . . . to the place that in Hebrew
is called Armageddon. (Rev. 16:13-14, 16)

The great day of God Almighty, the day of His wrath, is now identified
with the battle of Armageddon. In this battle,

> The beast was captured, and with him the false prophet . . . .
> The two of them were thrown alive into the fiery lake of burning
> sulfur. (Rev. 19:20)

To understand the significance of this battle, we need to know who
the "beast" and the "false prophet" represent. In chapters 8 and 9 of this
book, we found that the beast was identified as the papacy. But who is
the false prophet? The false prophet is identified with the "beast" that
"had two horns like a lamb" (Rev. 13:11).

> The beast with lamblike horns was seen "coming up out of the
> earth." Instead of overthrowing other powers to establish itself,
> the nation thus represented must arise in territory previously
> unoccupied and grow up gradually and peacefully. It could not,
> then, arise among the crowded and struggling nationalities of the
> Old World—that turbulent sea of "peoples, and multitudes, and
> nations, and tongues." It must be sought in the Western Continent.
> What nation of the New World was in 1798 rising into
> power, giving promise of strength and greatness, and attracting
> the attention of the world? The application of the symbol
> admits of no question. One nation, and only one, meets the
> specifications of this prophecy; it points unmistakably to the
> United States of America. (ibid., 440)

John says that the "false prophet" had performed "miraculous signs,"
and with "these signs he had deluded those who had received the mark
of the beast and worshiped his image" (Rev. 19:20).

We noticed in Revelation 13 that it is the beast out of the earth with
the two horns like a lamb that "performed great and miraculous signs"
with which "he deceived the inhabitants of the earth . . . . He also forced

everyone . . . to receive a mark on his right hand or on his forehead" (Rev. 13:14-16).

The involvement of the kings of the earth with the beast in this battle is further described in Revelation 17.

> The ten horns you saw are ten kings who have not yet received a kingdom, but who for one hour will receive authority as kings along with the beast. They will make war against the Lamb, but the Lamb will overcome them because he is Lord of lords and King of kings. (Rev. 17:12, 14)

In this battle, the kings of the earth who had joined the coalition (Rev. 16:13) "were killed with the sword that came out of the mouth of the rider on the horse, and all the birds gorged themselves on their flesh" (Rev. 19:21).

Before the battle is over, the dragon is captured. John writes,

> I saw an angel coming down out of heaven, having the key to the Abyss and holding in his hand a great chain. He seized the dragon, that ancient serpent, who is the devil, or Satan, and bound him for a thousand years. (Rev. 20:1-2)

The scriptures are very clear that Jesus will come the second time to fight the battle of Armageddon. But you may ask, "Why the battle?" What is the purpose of the great day of God's wrath and the treading of the winepress of God's fury? During the investigative judgment, October 22, 1844, to the close of probation, Jesus is determining, from the books of record, who from this earth will become subjects of the coming kingdom of glory. Although all the subjects are selected by the time probation closes, they will still be here on this earth, held captive by the dragon, the beast, the false prophet, and the kings of the earth. Soon after Christ finishes His mediatorial work and closes the sanctuary, His coronation as king over the kingdom of glory takes place in the celebration called the wedding of the Lamb.

> Having received the kingdom, He will come in His glory, as King of kings and Lord of lords, for the redemption of His people. (ibid., 427)

Jesus rides forth as a mighty conqueror. Not now a "Man of Sorrows," to drink the bitter cup of shame and woe, He comes, victor in heaven and earth, to judge the living and the dead. "Faithful and True," "in righteousness He doth judge and make war." And "the armies which were in heaven" (Revelation 19:11, 14) follow Him. With anthems of celestial melody the holy angels, a vast, unnumbered throng, attend Him on His way. The firmament seems filled with radiant forms . . . . No crown of thorns now mars that sacred head; but a diadem of glory rests on His holy brow. His countenance outshines the dazzling brightness of the noonday sun. "And He hath on His vesture and on His thigh a name written, *King of kings, and Lord of lords*." Revelation 19:16. (ibid., 641)

Such is the glory and splendor that surrounds the Savior when He comes to free the saints from the prison house of Satan.

The voice of the Son of God calls forth the sleeping saints. He looks upon the graves of the righteous, then, raising His hands to heaven, He cries: "Awake, awake, awake, ye that sleep in the dust, and arise!" . . . From the prison house of death they come, clothed with immortal glory, crying: "O death, where is thy sting? O grave, where is thy victory?" 1 Corinthians 15:55. And the living righteous and the risen saints unite their voices in a long, glad shout of victory. (ibid., 644)

The Lord himself will come down from heaven, with a loud command, with the voice of the archangel and with the trumpet call of God, and the dead in Christ will rise first. After that, we who are still alive and are left will be caught up together with them in the clouds to meet the Lord in the air. And so we will be with the Lord forever. (1 Thess. 4:16-17)

The living righteous are changed "in a moment, in the twinkling of an eye." At the voice of God they were glorified; now they are made immortal and with the risen saints are caught up to meet their Lord in the air.

On each side of the cloudy chariot are wings, and beneath it are living wheels; and as the chariot rolls upward, the wheels cry, "Holy," and the wings, as they move, cry, "Holy," and the retinue of angels cry, "Holy, holy, holy, Lord God Almighty." And the redeemed shout, "Alleluia!" as the chariot moves onward toward the New Jerusalem. (ibid., 645)

Thus ends the battle of Armageddon. The saints are on their way to the Holy City. All the wicked are dead, and Satan with his angels are bound to this desolate earth for 1,000 years.

Closing Events Time Line

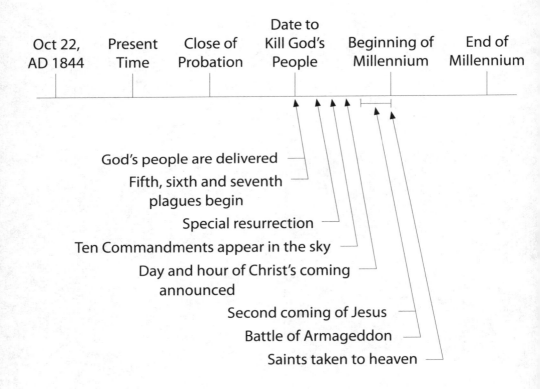

| Oct 22, AD 1844 | Present Time | Close of Probation | Date to Kill God's People | Beginning of Millennium | End of Millennium |

God's people are delivered

Fifth, sixth and seventh plagues begin

Special resurrection

Ten Commandments appear in the sky

Day and hour of Christ's coming announced

Second coming of Jesus

Battle of Armageddon

Saints taken to heaven

18

The Kingdom of Glory Restored

Oh, what a most wonderful journey for the subjects of the kingdom of glory as they travel heavenward from this earth to the Holy City, the New Jerusalem, with the victorious armies of the universe. Just outside the gates of the city, the procession stops.

Before entering the City of God, the Saviour bestows upon His followers the emblems of victory and invests them with the insignia of their royal state . . . . Upon the heads of the overcomers, Jesus with His own right hand places the crown of glory. For each there is a crown, bearing his own "new name" (Revelation 2:17), and the inscription, "Holiness to the Lord." In every hand are placed the victor's palm and the shining harp. Then, as the commanding angels strike the note, every hand sweeps the harp strings with skillful touch, awaking sweet music in rich, melodious strains. Rapture unutterable thrills every heart, and each voice is raised in grateful praise: "Unto Him that loved us, and washed us from our sins in His own blood, and hath made us kings and priests unto God and His Father; to Him be glory and dominion for ever and ever." Revelation 1:5, 6. (*The Great Controversy*, 645, 646)

With unutterable love, Jesus welcomes His faithful ones to the joy of their Lord. The Saviour's joy is in seeing, in the kingdom of glory, the souls that have been saved by His agony and humiliation. And the redeemed will be sharers in His joy, as they behold, among the blessed, those who have been won to Christ through their prayers, their labors, and their loving sacrifice. As they gather about the great white throne, gladness unspeakable will fill their hearts, when they behold those whom they have won for Christ, and see that one has gained others, and these still others, all brought into the haven of rest, there to lay their crowns at Jesus' feet and praise Him through the endless cycles of eternity. (ibid., 647)

Now the time has arrived for "His people, who are to 'sit down with Abraham, and Isaac, and Jacob,' at His table in His kingdom (Matthew 8:11; Luke 22:30), to partake of the marriage supper of the Lamb" (ibid., 427).

When this great feast is over, the saints begin their work of the executive judgment during which time "they will be priests of God and of Christ and will reign with him for a thousand years" (Rev. 20:6). In this judgment, the sentences are determined for all those who are lost and for Satan and his angels.

> At the close of the thousand years, Christ again returns to the earth. He is accompanied by the host of the redeemed and attended by a retinue of angels. As He descends in terrific majesty He bids the wicked dead arise to receive their doom. They come forth, a mighty host, numberless as the sands of the sea.
>
> Christ descends upon the Mount of Olives, whence, after His resurrection, He ascended, and where angels repeated the promise of His return. (ibid., 662)
>
> One of the seven angels who had the seven bowls full of the seven last plagues came and said to me, "Come, I will show you the bride, the wife of the Lamb." And he carried me away in the Spirit to a mountain great and high, and showed me the Holy City, Jerusalem, coming down out of heaven from God. (Rev. 21:9, 10)
>
> As the New Jerusalem, in its dazzling splendor, comes down out of heaven, it rests upon the place purified and made ready to receive it, and Christ, with His people and the angels, enters the Holy City.
>
> Now Satan prepares for a last mighty struggle for the supremacy . . . . As the wicked dead are raised and he sees the vast multitudes upon his side, his hopes revive, and he determines not to yield the great controversy . . . . He proposes to lead them against the camp of the saints and to take possession of the City of God. (ibid., 663)

In number they are like the sand on the seashore. They marched across the breadth of the earth and surrounded the camp of God's people, the city he loves. (Rev. 20:7-9)

Then I saw a great white throne and him who was seated on it. Earth and sky fled from his presence, and there was no place for them. (Rev. 20:11)

Now Christ again appears to the view of His enemies. Far above the city, upon a foundation of burnished gold, is a throne, high and lifted up. Upon this throne sits the Son of God, and around Him are the subjects of His kingdom. The power and majesty of Christ no language can describe, no pen portray. The glory of the Eternal Father is enshrouding His Son. The brightness of His presence fills the City of God, and flows out beyond the gates, flooding the whole earth with its radiance. (ibid., 665)

In the presence of the assembled inhabitants of earth and heaven the final coronation of the Son of God takes place. And now, invested with supreme majesty and power, the King of kings pronounces sentence upon the rebels against His government and executes justice upon those who have transgressed His law and oppressed His people. (ibid., 666)

John continues,

And I saw the dead, great and small, standing before the throne, and books were opened. Another book was opened, which is the book of life. The dead were judged according to what they had done as recorded in the books. (Rev. 20:12)

As soon as the books of record are opened, and the eye of Jesus looks upon the wicked, they are conscious of every sin which they have ever committed. They see just where their feet diverged from the path of purity and holiness, just how far pride and rebellion have carried them in the violation of the law of God. The seductive temptations which they encouraged by indulgence in sin, the blessings perverted, the messengers of God despised, the warnings rejected, the waves of mercy beaten back by the stubborn, unrepentant heart—all appear as if written in letters of fire. (ibid., 666)

John says, "The sea gave up the dead that were in it, and death and
Hades gave up the dead that were in them, and each person was judged
according to what he had done" (Rev. 20:13).

> The whole wicked world stand arraigned at the bar of
> God on the charge of high treason against the government of
> heaven. They have none to plead their cause; they are without
> excuse; and the sentence of eternal death is pronounced against
> them . . . .
>
> As if entranced, the wicked have looked upon the
> coronation of the Son of God. They see in His hands the tables
> of the divine law, the statutes which they have despised and
> transgressed. They witness the outburst of wonder, rapture, and
> adoration from the saved; and as the wave of melody sweeps
> over the multitudes without the city, all with one voice exclaim,
> "Great and marvelous are Thy works, Lord God Almighty;
> just and true are Thy ways, Thou King of saints" (Revelation
> 15:3); and, falling prostrate, they worship the Prince of life.
> (ibid., 668-669)
>
> The time has now come when the rebellion is to be finally
> defeated and the history and character of Satan disclosed. In
> his last great effort to dethrone Christ, destroy His people,
> and take possession of the City of God, the archdeceiver has
> been fully unmasked. Those who have united with him see
> the total failure of his cause. Christ's followers and the loyal
> angels behold the full extent of his machinations against the
> government of God. He is the object of universal abhorrence.
> (ibid., 670)
>
> His power is at an end. The wicked are filled with the same
> hatred of God that inspires Satan; but they see that their case is
> hopeless, that they cannot prevail against Jehovah. Their rage
> is kindled against Satan and those who have been his agents in
> deception, and with the fury of demons they turn upon them.
> (ibid., 672)

"But fire came down from heaven and devoured them." "Then death
and Hades were thrown into the lake of fire. The lake of fire is the second
death. If anyone's name was not found written in the book of life, he was
thrown into the lake of fire." (Rev 20:9, last part, 14, 15)

And the devil, who deceived them, was thrown into the lake of burning sulfur, where the beast and the false prophet had been thrown. They will be tormented day and night for ever and ever. (Rev 20:10)

Fire comes down from God out of heaven. The earth is broken up. The weapons concealed in its depths are drawn forth. Devouring flames burst from every yawning chasm. The very rocks are on fire. The day has come that shall burn as an oven. The elements melt with fervent heat, the earth also, and the works that are therein are burned up. Malachi 4:1; 2 Peter 3:10. The earth's surface seems one molten mass—a vast, seething lake of fire. It is the time of the judgment and perdition of ungodly men—"the day of the Lord's vengeance, and the year of recompenses for the controversy of Zion." Isaiah 34:8.

The wicked receive their recompense in the earth. Proverbs 11:31. They "shall be stubble: and the day that cometh shall burn them up, saith the Lord of hosts." Malachi 4:1. Some are destroyed as in a moment, while others suffer many days. All are punished "according to their deeds." The sins of the righteous having been transferred to Satan, he is made to suffer not only for his own rebellion, but for all the sins which he has caused God's people to commit. His punishment is to be far greater than that of those whom he has deceived. After all have perished who fell by his deceptions, he is still to live and suffer on. In the cleansing flames the wicked are at last destroyed, root and branch—Satan the root, his followers the branches. The full penalty of the law has been visited; the demands of justice have been met; and heaven and earth, beholding, declare the righteousness of Jehovah. (ibid., 672-673)

The fire that consumes the wicked purifies the earth. Every trace of the curse is swept away. No eternally burning hell will keep before the ransomed the fearful consequences of sin.

One reminder alone remains: Our Redeemer will ever bear the marks of His crucifixion. Upon His wounded head, upon His side, His hands and feet, are the only traces of the cruel work that sin has wrought. Says the prophet, beholding Christ in His glory: "He had bright beams coming out of His side: and there was the hiding of His power." Habakkuk 3:4, margin. That pierced side whence flowed the crimson stream that reconciled man to God—there is the Saviour's glory, there "the hiding of His power." "Mighty to save," through the sacrifice of redemption, He was therefore strong to execute justice upon them that despised God's mercy. And the tokens of His humiliation are His highest honor; through the eternal ages the wounds of Calvary will show forth His praise and declare His power . . . .

God's original purpose in the creation of the earth is fulfilled as it is made the eternal abode of the redeemed. "The righteous shall inherit the land, and dwell therein forever." Psalm 37:29. (ibid., 674)

The great controversy is ended. Sin and sinners are no more. The entire universe is clean. One pulse of harmony and gladness beats through the vast creation. From Him who created all, flow life and light and gladness, throughout the realms of illimitable space. From the minutest atom to the greatest world, all things, animate and inanimate, in their unshadowed beauty and perfect joy, declare that God is love. (ibid., 678)

Closing Events Time Line

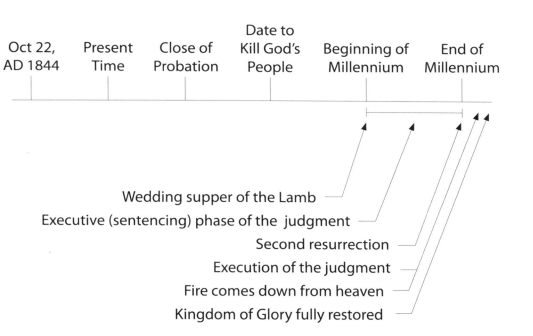

For Further Study

To enroll for a correspondence course on Bible prophecy concerning end-time events, contact

Maurice Hoppe, Director
Revelation Ministry
9340 E. Prairie Meadows Circle
Derby, KS 67037
(316) 789-0625
hoppe@revelationministry.com

To learn more about the wondrous plan of salvation and God's gracious purpose for mankind, sign up now for the Foundation and Pillars of the Christian Faith correspondence course. Just write, email or call

Steps to Life
PO Box 782828
Wichita, KS 67278
1-800-843-8788
info@stepstolife.org